WAY

TRUTH

LIFE

Discipleship
as a Journey
of Grace

David A. Busic

THE FOUNDRY
PUBLISHING

Also by David A. Busic

Perfectly Imperfect: Character Sketches from the Old Testament (2013)
Perfectly Imperfect: Character Sketches from the New Testament (2014)
The City: Urban Churches in the Wesleyan-Holiness Tradition (2020)

Praise for *Way, Truth, Life*

Way, Truth, Life is not just another discipleship book to add to the stack. It is a journey adaptable to the global context. David Busic takes the reader to the depths and joys of understanding the meaning of grace—the missing ingredient in the book market today. Busic's writing is compelling, weaving a biblical foundation with historical and theological principles and current-day experiences of grace. The great hope throughout the book will bring renewal to a hungry world.

Jo Anne Lyon
Ambassador and General Superintendent Emerita
The Wesleyan Church

When denominational leadership decided to commission a book that would present our theology and philosophy on discipleship, we immediately thought of Dr. David Busic for this work. We needed someone with the ability to provide sound theological foundation and practical applications to the new denominational framework envisioned by the Board of General Superintendents. This book provides a contemporary summation of our essential doctrines as they apply to the practice of discipleship, both globally and at the local church levels. We believe this book will serve generations to come as we fulfill our mission "to make Christlike disciples in the nations."

Gustavo Crocker
General Superintendent
Church of the Nazarene

Grace—the unmerited and unending favor of God toward all people—is not only amazing but also deep and potentially complex. In his uniquely gifted way, Busic clarifies, simplifies, and celebrates the multifaceted diamond that is God's grace. However, more than a head-directed theological exploration of the many dimensions of grace, this book serves as a heart invitation to live into God's grace in ways that have not only "brought us safe thus far" but also that will "lead us home" into God's grace-filled new creation.

Scott Daniels
Lead Pastor
Nampa (ID) College Church of the Nazarene

Way, Truth, Life is a thoroughly Wesleyan-Holiness guide for those participating in the Great Commission, both from the perspective of becoming
a disciple and of being a disciple maker. The role of sanctifying grace is
a crucial centerpiece of this work, encouraging all readers to continually
grow in truth. Busic has provided the church a gift through this theologically
informed resource for discipleship in the twenty-first century.

Carla Sunberg
General Superintendent
Church of the Nazarene

Way, Truth, Life is a profound, comprehensive understanding of God's unself-
ish love displayed in Jesus Christ, the full image of his being. Busic biblically
and theologically describes how God encounters us in all the stages of life,
graciously offering himself through Christ, restoring us to his eternal purpose of full fellowship with him. Our journey with God through Christ is an
intimate relationship of grace. Busic contributes to the church as the body
of Christ, bringing it back to its Wesleyan roots and aiming to launch every
believer on the journey of grace together, demonstrating Christ and expand-
ing the kingdom of God.

Christian Sarmiento
South America Regional Director
Church of the Nazarene

I have been on a few trips before. When I went alone, I was lonely, often
lost and consequently late. Had I a companion and a correct map, it could
have been so different. On your trip, I suggest you take Busic's *Way, Truth,
Life* because these pages will tenderly lead you to a divine Companion.
Once you finish reading it and discover for yourself the transforming truth
therein, you will never want to travel alone again.

Robert Broadbooks
USA/Canada Regional Director
Church of the Nazarene

Combining a Wesleyan-Holiness theology of grace with a practical focus
on the journey of discipleship, Busic calls every follower of Jesus to a life
marked by ever-increasing Christlikeness. A true gift to Christ's church! Join
the journey, and bring someone along.

Scott Rainey
Global Director of Sunday School and Discipleship Ministries
Church of the Nazarene

Cover Design: Matt Johnson
Interior Design: Sharon Page

Library of Congress Cataloging-in-Publication Data
Names: Busic, David A., 1964- author.
Title: Way, truth, life : discipleship as a journey of grace / David A. Busic.
Description: Kansas City, MO : The Foundry Publishing, 2021. | Includes bibliographical references. |
    Summary: "In Way, Truth, Life, David Busic invites you as you invite others to join a global campaign to discover together the various ways that God's seeking, saving, sanctifying, sustaining, and sufficient grace meets us where we are in our lives. If we respond faithfully to the One who lovingly calls and equips us for the Journey of Grace, we will gain a deeper relationship with Jesus Christ, who is himself the Way, the Truth, and the Life"— Provided by publisher.
Identifiers: LCCN 2020023953 (print) | LCCN 2020023954 (ebook) | ISBN 9780834139695 |
    ISBN 9780834139701 (ebook)
Subjects: LCSH: Spiritual formation. | Grace (Theology)
Classification: LCC BV4511 .B87 2021 (print) | LCC BV4511 (ebook) | DDC 248.4—dc23
LC record available at https://lccn.loc.gov/2020023953
LC ebook record available at https://lccn.loc.gov/2020023954

10 9 8 7 6 5 4 3 2 1

In memory of Robert E. Busic, a father who taught me
that discipleship is a journey suffused by grace and
that Christlikeness is our destiny.

Teach me your way, O LORD, that I may walk in your truth;
give me an undivided heart to revere your name.
—Psalm 86:11

CONTENTS

ACKNOWLEDGMENTS

Acknowledgments can span the range from recognition of those who make something possible to debts of gratitude that cannot be repaid. So it is now.

When I was elected to serve as a general superintendent for the Church of the Nazarene, I knew my colleagues on the Board of General Superintendents would impact my life, but the degree of their influence has been inestimable. While there are almost always differences of opinion in our innumerable leadership conversations, the things that remain steadfast are their commitment to faithfully and prayerfully doing what is best for the church—even when it is costly —and my absolute trust in the strength of their character and purity of their hearts. Thank you to Filimao Chambo, Gustavo Crocker, Eugenio Duarte, David Graves, Jerry Porter, Carla Sunberg, and J. K. Warrick. Your influence has inspired the writing of this book in service to the church to help us fulfill our mission "to make Christlike disciples in the nations."

Thank you to Scott Rainey, director of global discipleship ministries for the Church of the Nazarene, for the invitation to write a simple book that emphasizes holiness discipleship as a journey of grace. Thank you to Bonnie Perry, director of editorial at The Foundry Publishing, for her unwavering belief that good theology written down and passed along to our children is a task important enough to invest her best life. Thank you to Audra Spiven for editing with an eye for clarity and always asking the question, "What if you said it this way?"

Finally, thank you to the not overly large in attendance but extravagantly loving Nazarene congregation of my youth, who taught me that holiness is not only what God in Christ has done for us but also what God in Christ is relentlessly doing in us and through us when we give up the right to ourselves and let Jesus be Lord.

Note from the Author

As has been my style in previous writings, I encourage the reader to consult the copious footnotes for a greater breadth of understanding regarding discipleship and the journey of grace. The abundant annotations reflect my debt to the thinking of others and my desire to offer additional insights that would be a burden to the main body of the text. For the sake of accessibility, full citations are offered each time a new chapter begins, even if that author or resource has been acknowledged before.

INTRODUCTION

Jesus invites us to a journey. "Come, follow me." It is a simple invitation to go on an adventure with a beloved friend. The Christian life is more than right belief. It is more than intellectual assent. It is an invitation to a journey with Jesus.

Another word for the journey with Jesus is discipleship. Discipleship, following the *way* of Jesus *with* Jesus, has many twists and turns and unexpected bends in the road. Sometimes the path feels easy and other times like a demanding incline. But the end goal (in Greek, *telos*) of discipleship is always the same: to be like Christ.

If that seems impossible, you are actually in a very good place to start. In fact, it *would* be impossible if it were not for a very important certainty: we make the journey *with Jesus*. That is why it is a journey of grace.

When Jesus said, "I am the way, and the truth, and the life" (John 14:6), he was talking about more than a sequential intellectual equation or a transactional agreement we make with God. He was describing the relational way discipleship will happen. Indeed, Way, Truth, and Life are not philosophical abstractions or life principles. Way, Truth, and Life are a Person.

Jesus was pointing toward the proper *telos* (goal) of the journey: real *life* as God intended, and the means by which we reach the goal are the *way* and the *truth*, fulfilled in and through himself.[1] The journey of grace is relational to the core.

James K. A. Smith describes discipleship as "a kind of immigration, from the kingdom of darkness to the kingdom of God's beloved Son (Col. 1:13)."[2] This is journey language—moving from one country to another.[3] It is about changing citizenship and allegiances, which is entirely impossible apart from the grace of God in Jesus Christ, who is the Way. Smith continues: "In Christ we are given a heavenly passport; in his body we learn to live like 'locals' of his kingdom. Such an immigration to a new kingdom isn't just a matter of being teleported to a different realm; we need to be acclimated to a new way of life, learn a new language, acquire new habits—and unlearn the habits of that rival dominion."[4]

I really believe that when Jesus said, "I am going to prepare a place for you" (John 14), that promise included the guarantee that he has personally made reservations for the trip, including accommodations when we arrive. He is our heavenly passport who enables us to become locals of a new country—of his kingdom. Best of all, he promises to accompany us all the way home. Jesus will be our Way for the way. This is the hope of a journey of grace.

I Am the Way, and the Truth, and the Life

When Jesus said, "I am the way, and the truth, and the life," he wasn't suggesting an abstract life principle to hang on the wall. Rather, it was a response to a question raised by scared and uncertain

---

1. Richard John Neuhaus defines *telos* as "the ultimate end that gives meaning to the thing in question." Neuhaus, *Death on a Friday Afternoon: Meditations on the Last Words of Jesus from the Cross* (New York: Basic Books, 2000), 127.

2. James K. A. Smith, *You Are What You Love: The Spiritual Power of Habit* (Grand Rapids: Brazos Press, 2016), 66.

3. John Bunyan's *The Pilgrim's Progress* (1678) was a fictional early version of this same concept of the journey one takes to change countries/kingdoms.

4. Smith, *You Are What You Love*, 66.

disciples. It comes from a section in the Gospel of John that biblical scholars refer to as The Last Discourse (John 14–17). These four chapters of John, more than any of the other New Testament Gospels, give us an inside look into what Jesus was thinking about and teaching his disciples during the hours just before his Passion and death on the cross. Thus, they could well be described as the last will and testament of Jesus Christ.[5]

Remember, the disciples have just heard incredibly *bad news*. They have gathered in a borrowed room. Everyone is packed into tight quarters. Jesus washes his twelve disciples' feet, which makes everyone uncomfortable. Then he proceeds to tell them that very soon one of them will betray him (13:21). To make matters worse, after several years of traveling everywhere together, Jesus tells them that he is leaving and that they cannot go with him (13:33).

This is all very upsetting! Jesus can feel the weight of his words settling over them. No wonder he says, "Do not let your hearts be troubled" (14:1). The word translated as "troubled" is the same word used to describe the waters of the Sea of Galilee during a raging storm. When the wind blew, the waters became choppy and churning. The disciples are feeling like that. Their stomachs are churning. Their heads are spinning. Their emotions are on overload. Jesus tries to comfort their raging hearts: "Do not let your hearts be troubled . . . I go to prepare a place for you . . . I will come again and will take you to myself, so that where I am, there you may be also. And you know the way to the place where I am going" (vv. 1a, 2b, 3b–4).

Then Thomas speaks up. History has named him Doubting Thomas, but I am glad he was there because Thomas has the cour-

---

5. Frederick Dale Bruner refers to John 14–16 as Jesus's discipleship sermons, with chapter 17 serving as a closing prayer and, taken altogether, "Jesus's compact systematic theology for his missionary church." Bruner, *The Gospel of John: A Commentary* (Grand Rapids: Eerdmans, 2012), 786.

age to ask the question everyone else wanted an answer to. He is like a student in a classroom who stops the professor in the middle of the lecture and says, "Excuse me. This may sound silly, but we have no idea what you're talking about right now." In fact, it wasn't a silly question. I can appreciate the fact that Thomas had the presence of mind to identify the large elephant in the room and ask the pressing question on everyone's mind: "Lord, we do not know where you are going. How can we know the way?" (v. 5).

Life is like that, isn't it? There are times when we find ourselves wondering which way to turn. Times when we thought we knew where we were going—or *hoped* we knew where we were going—but having to admit we'd completely lost our way. There seem to be so many intersections and turns, so many options and dead ends. What we wish for more than anything else in the puzzle of life is a map. However, many people, not finding that map, decide it's better to go somewhere than stay nowhere, so they pick a direction and head off on whatever seems to be the path of least resistance.

Thankfully, Jesus answers Thomas's question (and ours): "I am the way, and the truth, and the life. No one comes to the Father except through me" (v. 6). It's interesting that the emphasis of Jesus's claim is clearly on "the way." The way is sequentially first. That is not to say that the truth and the life are not important. It simply means that the truth and the life explain *how* and *why* Jesus is the Way.[6]

He is the Way because he is the Truth—the revelation of God. He is the Way because the life of God available to every person resides in him and him alone. He is simultaneously both the *access to*

<hr/>

6. Considered by many to be the preeminent Johannine scholar of his generation, Raymond Brown believes, "*the way* is the primary predicate [of the statement of Jesus], and *the truth* and *the life* are just explanations of the way." Brown, *The Gospel According to John XII-XXI, The Anchor Bible Commentary* (New York: Doubleday, 1970), 621. If this is correct, the truth and the life are explanations of the way—or, said differently, Jesus is the Way because he is the Truth and the Life. Jesus personally embodies all three.

and the *embodiment of* life with God. The heart of the good news of John's Gospel is that in Jesus—the incarnate Word and unique Son of God—we can see and know God in a manner never before made possible. He is the authorized self-disclosure of God.[7] In other words, Jesus is not merely *a* way but *the* way—because he is the exceptional, visible manifestation of the invisible God whom we know as Father (1:14, 18; 6:46; 8:19; 12:45).[8]

"No one comes to the Father except through me" (14:6). Many of us can relate to Thomas's question, "How can we know the way?" (v. 5) because every person, whether articulated or not, is searching for answers to spiritual questions. Our society today is more spiritually open than it has been in many years. The problem is that people are open to many different avenues of spirituality.

The modern Western worldview—drawing from an all-encompassing consumer mentality and linked with the very recent political concern for gracious plurality—causes many to view one spiritual path to be just as relevant and legitimate as any other, as long as our personal needs are being met, and as long as we are being authentically true to our own selves. And so it is assumed—whether one chooses Buddhism, Hinduism, Islam, Scientology, Judaism, Christianity, or any other religion—that, as long as one is sincere and is gratified by one's choice, then that alternative is as good as any other because all paths lead (so the worldview says) to the same God.

One of the many problems with such a view is that these different beliefs often contradict each other and make mutually exclusive claims. When Christianity is viewed in light of the many other di-

---

7. Bruner, *The Gospel of John*, 811. Bruner reminds us that "Jesus's disclosure of God the Father gives us great hope that the Father too [like Jesus] will be—and, indeed, is and always has been—very, very good."

8. I draw inspiration for this sentence from a poetic footnote in *The Wesley Study Bible: New Revised Standard Version*, Joel B. Green and William H. Willimon, eds. (Nashville: Abingdon Press, 2009).

verse religious systems, it is the only faith that makes the definitive claim that Jesus is the exclusive way to God. One cannot believe in Jesus Christ's exclusive claim, "No one comes to the Father except through me," and still maintain that there are other ways to gain access to the Father. In effect, to do so would deny the very Christ who spoke those words. Jesus did not say, "I am one of many ways to the Father." He did not say, "You can choose to follow me if you like, but there are other choices that are just as viable." Nor did Jesus say, "Whichever spiritual path you walk down will be fine with me, as long as you're sincere." Jesus never even hinted at that. He stated clearly that he is the only way to the Father.[9]

Not long after our family moved to a new city, my wife and I had an appointment across town. We had to take separate vehicles. Because her sense of direction has always been better than mine, she led the way. Suddenly we were caught in dense traffic, and I lost her. I thought I was following her, but by the time I realized I wasn't, I was on a completely different road, and it was too late even to get to the appointment. I simply turned around and went home. The moral of the story is simple: You can be sincere in the path you choose and simultaneously be sincerely wrong. The fact is, it takes more than sincerity to find the right way.[10] It takes truth! A person can be making good time in the direction they are going, but if it's the wrong way, it doesn't matter how quickly they arrive.

Jesus's claim is radically *inclusive* because all are invited to follow the way, but it is radically *exclusive* in that every path a person follows

---

9. This is not to limit the sovereignty of God to graciously reach adherents of other religions and faith traditions who may die without knowing or even hearing the name of Jesus. God is always free to do that which God sovereignly chooses to do. I fully expect to be surprised by grace in the reconciliation of all things.

10. No one is more sincere about their truth than suicide bombers. However, sincerity—no matter how passionately committed one is to their truth—is not enough if it isn't grounded in ultimate reality.

to find the truth winds up as a dead end—unless it is the one Way that leads them to the one true God.

Every person—every single one of us—is guilty of taking the wrong turn, spiritually speaking. As a result, we find ourselves far from God. The prophet Isaiah pointedly writes: "All we like sheep have gone astray; we have all turned to our own way" (53:6a). The apostle Paul reiterates in Romans, "All have sinned and fall short of the glory of God" (3:23). Why? Because we have all taken the wrong road in life. We have all chosen to follow our own way instead of pursuing God's will and way for our lives.

The gospel (good news) is that Jesus came for people like us. Another Gospel writer, Luke, tells us that Jesus's stated mission purpose is "to seek out and to save the lost" (19:10). Rather than leaving us standing indecisively at a fork in the road, or worse, aimlessly following the wrong path entirely, Jesus came to show us clearly the only way to God, to the new country of the kingdom, and to eternal life.

One commentator paraphrases Jesus's words this way: "I, I am the Way there, and I, I am the Truth that will lead you on the Way there, and I, I am the Life that will give you the power to follow the Truth along the Way there."[11] Not a set of directions, not a roadmap, not a set of clues—I AM[12] the Way. Not a set of life-organizing principles or philosophical presuppositions—I AM the Truth. Not an alternative way to live with a more optimistic viewpoint—I AM the only real Life, the singular means to becoming truly human.

This claim of Jesus Christ to be not merely *a* way, and *a* truth, and *a* life, but to be the true and unique Son of God, is the bedrock of

---

11. Bruner, *The Gospel of John*, 823.

12. The pronoun [*ego*, "I"] is emphatic, turning the emphasis from a method to a Person. It is also noteworthy, and has been highlighted innumerable times, that Jesus's "I AM" sayings in John are a not-so-subtle reference to God's burning bush pronouncement to Moses, "I AM WHO I AM" (Exod. 3:14). "I AM" became known throughout the Hebrew scriptures as *Yahweh*.

Christianity. That is not to malign other faith systems; it is simply to say there is only one way to the Father, and it is through Jesus Christ. He is the only means by which we may be saved. As Frederick Bruner has pointed out, "The East has perennially longed for 'the Way' (the *Tao*), the West for 'the Truth' (*Veritas*), and the whole world (east, west, north, and south) for 'the (*real*) Life.' Jesus is, in person, all three."[13]

Imagine you are in an unfamiliar town and you ask someone for directions to a particular destination. The person you asked for help could say, "You have to veer to the right at the next big intersection. Then cross the square, go past the church, stay in the middle lane, which will take you directly to the third street on the right, until you come to a four-lane stop." Even with clear guidance, when the way is complicated, the chances of making a wrong turn or getting lost are fairly high.

Suppose that instead, the person you ask says, "You know, there is no easy way to get there. It is fairly complicated if you have never been there before. Just follow me. Better yet, *come with me*, and I'll take you there." That person not only becomes your guide, but they also essentially become the way, and you cannot miss getting where you need to go. That is what Jesus does for us. He doesn't just give advice and directions. He walks with us on a journey of grace. Indeed, he does not tell us about the way—he becomes the Way!

British theologian and renowned missiologist Lesslie Newbigin powerfully articulated this perspective: "It is not that he [Jesus] teaches the way, or guides us in the way: if that were so, we could thank him for his teaching and then proceed to follow it on our own. He himself *is* the way. . . . To follow this way is, in fact, the only way to the Father."[14]

---

13. Bruner, *The Gospel of John*, 812.

14. Lesslie Newbigin, *The Light Has Come: An Exposition of the Fourth Gospel* (Grand Rapids: Eerdmans, 1987), 181. Emphasis added.

In Lewis Carroll's *Alice's Adventures in Wonderland*, Alice comes to a crossroads and asks the Cheshire Cat a question: "Would you tell me, please, which way I ought to go from here?"

"That depends a good deal on where you want to go," answers the Cat.

"I don't much care where I go," Alice replies.

"Then it doesn't matter which way you go," said the Cat.

Perhaps no one has more eloquently summarized Jesus's unique claim than Thomas à Kempis in his devotional classic, *Of the Imitation of Christ*:

Follow thou me: "I am the way, the truth, and the life." Without the way, there is no going; without the truth, there is no knowing; without the life, there is no living. I am the way, which thou oughtest to follow; the truth, which thou oughtest to trust; the life, which thou oughtest to hope for. I am the way inviolable, the truth infallible, the life that cannot end. If thou remain in my way, thou shalt know the truth, and the truth shall make thee free, and thou shalt lay hold on eternal life.[15]

In Jesus, we find the Way to the Father. He is the way home.

In Jesus, we find the Truth. He embodies the unchanging, sure, and certain truth of the character and nature of the Father.

In Jesus, we find Life—abundant life, both now and in the promised new creation of God to come.

This is the journey of grace.

---

15. Thomas à Kempis, *Of the Imitation of Christ*, Book 3, chapter 56 (c. 1418–1427).

1
AMAZING GRACE

Grace is everywhere.
—Georges Bernanos, *The Diary of a Country Priest*

"Amazing Grace" is one of the most famous and beloved songs in the world today. Although it is more than two centuries old, it continues to be sung in hundreds of languages and dialects.[1] It transcends race and creed, geographical and generational boundaries. You don't even have to be a Christian to know the words and be moved by their meaning.

An English pastor named John Newton wrote the song. During the early part of his adult life, he was the captain of a slave ship and was responsible for bringing hundreds of slaves from West Africa to Great Britain. However, following a near-death encounter during a violent storm at sea, he had a conversion experience that radically changed him. He would never be the same.

Not only did he begin a journey of grace with God, but he also came to deeply regret and repent of his personal involvement in the

---

1. As I write this sitting in an airport lounge in Johannesburg, South Africa, I can hear one of the workers humming it softly in Afrikaans. American journalist Bill Moyers was attending a performance at Lincoln Center where the audience sang "Amazing Grace." He was so impressed by the unifying power of the song, among Christians and non-Christians alike, that he was inspired to produce a documentary by the same name.

slave trade. He resigned his captainship, became an Anglican pastor, and later came to be a mentor to William Wilberforce, who led the campaign to abolish slavery in the British Empire. At the age of eighty-two, as he lay dying, Newton declared, "My memory is nearly gone. But I remember two things: that I am a great sinner, and that Christ is a great Saviour." No wonder he could write so poetically—he had received, experienced, and been transformed by amazing grace.

This is a book about grace. It is about the journey of grace by which we are made more and more into the image of Jesus Christ, who is the Way, the Truth, and the Life. Grace comes in many forms, both in Scripture and in our lives, but the nature of grace remains the same. We receive it personally as a gift from God and cooperate with God within a mutual and transforming relationship.

What Is Grace?

What is God's grace? How does it come into our lives, affect us, change us, and empower us to live Christlike lives? There are many definitions of grace:

- God's unmerited favor.
- God's undeserved love.
- The favor given to someone who deserves the opposite.
- The absolutely free expression of the love of God finding its only motive in the bounty and benevolence of the Giver.[2]
- God's no-strings-attached goodness.

All of these definitions for grace attempt to describe those indescribable and astounding aspects of God's loving response to undeserving humanity. This is why we use the word "amazing." It defies our human categories of relationships and transactions.

---

2. This is a loose paraphrase of the definition of grace attributed to now-deceased New Testament scholar, linguist, and missions leader Spiros Zodhiates.

Those in the world of finance know what a "grace period" is. Grace periods are small windows of time when what someone owes to a lending company is deferred without penalty. When a loan is deferred without incurring late fees, that is a grace period—but there *are* strings attached. It only lasts for a short time (it is a grace *period*). Eventually, it will be over, and if someone still has not paid what they owe, they will be charged additional penalties. It is free—but it is not unconditional.

God's grace is different. God's grace comes free of charge (not to be confused with "no cost"—more on this idea at the end of the chapter), and it is a good thing it does because we could not afford it anyway. We could never pay or repay what we owe to God. It is by his grace that God does for us what we could never do for ourselves. That is why we say grace is unmerited and undeserved. God treats us better than we deserve. It is the favor given to us when we deserve the opposite, and that compels us to follow Jesus in thoroughly devoted discipleship.

The simplest definition of grace is "gift." The apostle Paul borrowed the common Greek word for "gift" or "favor," *charis*, and helped reimagine it as a way to describe the vast meaning of all that God has done for us in Jesus Christ (2 Cor. 8:9; 9:15; Gal. 2:21; Eph. 2:4–10).[3] It is also important to note that *charis* is derived from the root *char*—"that which brings joy."[4] Thus, the action of grace given and received evokes both joy and gratitude. In that sense, it is appropriate for recipients of grace to offer something in return: thanksgiving and a consecrated life. This does not imply that divine grace is a relational transaction. The desire (or expectation) to repay the favor

---

3. The Greek word *charis* is translated in Latin as *gratia*, or simply, "grace."

4. Thomas A. Langford, *Reflections on Grace* (Eugene, OR: Cascade Books, 2007), 28.

negates the power of the gift.[5] Transactional thinking always undermines and devalues the intentions of a gift.

If I give my friend a gift, I might say, "I want to give this gift as a sign of my love for you."

The normal response would be for my friend to receive the gift and simply say, "Thank you."

What if, instead, my friend said, "That is very nice of you. How much do I owe you?" He has then moved the language of a gift into the language of a transaction: *You are doing something nice for me. I owe you one.*

There is another problem with conflating the gift of grace with transactions that are repayable. The underlying meaning of grace is that there is nothing we can do to make God love us more and nothing we can do to make God love us less than he already does.[6] There is nothing so good about us that makes us worthy or able to earn God's love, and there is nothing so bad about us that can separate us from the love of God, which is in Christ Jesus our Lord (Rom. 8:35–39). God doesn't love us because we are good, and God doesn't hate us because we are bad. God's essential nature is holy love, which means God's characteristic action is divinely self-giving, poured-out grace.[7]

---

5. In *Paul and the Gift* (Grand Rapids: Eerdmans, 2015), John M. G. Barkley makes a strong case that the idea of "gift" as something handed over "gratuitously, for nothing" is a modern Western concept. Throughout antiquity, and even today in many parts of the world, gifts are given with strong expectations of return—even in order to gain something that would strengthen social solidarity. The New Testament Gospel understanding of the "gift" of salvation is that, while it is not deserved and cannot be earned, grace begets righteousness, and righteousness begets obedience.

6. Philip Yancey, *What's So Amazing about Grace?* (Grand Rapids: Zondervan, 1997), 70.

7. "God's most essential characteristic is love. 'God is love,' John says simply yet most profoundly. We may modify God's love with the word 'holy.' However, this adds little to an understanding of God because, by nature, God's love is holy. The modifier 'holy' does remind us, however, that God is beyond us as other than us. God is holy and always different from us in nature." Diane LeClerc, *Discovering Christian Holiness: The*

Philip Yancey gets at this when he writes: "Grace means that God already loves us as much as an infinite God can possibly love."[8] Since God did not initially love us based on our good behavior, how could better behavior make God love us more? Similarly, how could worse behavior make God love us less? You cannot pray more, give more, serve more, or sacrifice more and cause God to say, "She is doing so much better. She is finally getting herself together. I love her more now than I did before." No. You are loved as you are. Everything does *not* depend on what you do or how you behave—not because you deserve it but because this is the first and last inclination of the heart of God.

A common comparison between justice, mercy, and grace says it well: Justice is getting what you deserve. Mercy is not getting what you deserve. Grace is getting what you do not deserve.

Jesus told many parables to help us reimagine life from a kingdom point of view. These parables were not just moral stories told to show us a better way to live. They help us better understand, and correct, our concept of the nature and heart of God. Think about the parables of the lost sheep, lost coin, and lost sons (Luke 15).[9] Jesus describes God as a shepherd who is overjoyed not because ninety-nine sheep followed the rules but because one of his own who was lost has been found. He describes God as a woman who turns her house upside down in search of a precious coin. When she finds it, she is so ecstatic that she throws a party to celebrate with her friends. Then he describes God as a lovesick father who searches the horizon for signs of a wayward son. When he spots the wandering boy "while he was still far off" (Luke 15:20), he is filled with compassion and runs

---

Heart of Wesleyan-Holiness Theology (Kansas City, MO: Beacon Hill Press of Kansas City, 2010), 274.

8. Yancey, *What's So Amazing about Grace?*, 70.

9. My use of "sons" in the plural is intentional. Jesus's teaching in this parable seems clear that both sons were lost for different reasons—but only one left home.

to welcome him home. These are all insights into the nature and heart of God. *Foundness* delights the heart of God! Grace overcomes wandering, lostness, and infidelity.

Jesus told another parable about laborers in a vineyard whose employer pays all the workers the same wage even though some worked far fewer hours than others (Matt. 20:1–16). This story makes no economic sense. It seems like an unwise business practice. This kind of reckless behavior from business owners runs the risk of alienating the hardest-working employees and encouraging laziness from the less motivated—but this isn't a parable about best business practices; it is a parable about the extravagant grace of God. Grace is not a mathematical equation that keeps a tally of employee hours, follows proper accounting principles, or rewards the hardest workers. Grace is not about who deserves to be paid; it is about *undeserving* persons who are given gifts anyway. If this sounds scandalous to your ears and ludicrous to your common sense, then you are beginning to get the point of grace.

Grace Is Personal

We can speak of the *experience* of grace because it is profoundly personal and relational. Grace is personal for two important reasons. First, grace is not a *thing*. It is not a commodity. It is not a holy substance poured into us like Christian motor oil to help our discipleship engine run more efficiently. Grace is personal because it comes to us in the *person* of Jesus Christ, who said, "I am the way, and the truth, and the life."[10]

---

10. When the Gospel of John speaks of the Holy Spirit as "another" Advocate, it means that the Spirit of Truth will continue the ministry of Jesus the Truth (14:6, 16–17).

Thomas Langford, a theologian in the Wesleyan tradition, maintains that throughout the history of the church there has been a struggle between two understandings of grace:

On the one hand, grace has been thought of as some *thing*, some thing God possesses and can give, and perhaps some thing persons can accept and possess; or, in larger terms, some atmosphere, energy, or power which represents God's action and provides a surrounding context for human life. On the other hand, grace has been identified with some *one*; grace is a person, grace is God— God present to human beings. To speak of grace is to speak of God's presence and caring interaction with creation. In this understanding, considerations of grace are based upon reflections on the life, death, and resurrection of Jesus. Jesus Christ is grace; grace is Jesus Christ.[11]

I am struck by the power of Diarmaid MacCulloch's weighty statement in his monumental history of Christianity: "A *person*, not a system, captured [Paul] in the mysterious events on the road to Damascus."[12] In so many ways, Saul of Tarsus—later renamed Paul the apostle—was not prepared for this astonishing revelation. His commitment had been to a religion, a defined system, a tradition, a Law. He knew it all too well. He was its trained and passionate defender—but it was a *person* who changed him. That person was Jesus of Nazareth, whom Paul would later identify as Christ and Lord.

Paul's previous belief system was total adherence to the Law. After the Damascus road experience (Acts 9:1–22), he saw things differently. He still believed the Law was good—but incomplete. When he met the Person, he turned his focus from what was good (his Jewish heritage) to some*one* incomparably better: *Jesus Christ*. Through

---

11. Langford, *Reflections on Grace*, 18.

12. Diarmaid MacCulloch, *Christianity: The First Three Thousand Years* (New York: Penguin Books, 2009), 99.

the experience of an intimate meeting with Christ, he discovered a righteousness that was not his own.[13] Paul believed that the relationship of the believer to Christ (the Person) could become so intimate that he speaks of it as "oneness in Christ," indicating total union. Oneness was not an abstract Greco-Roman, Platonic concept for Paul. Jesus Christ was (is) a real human being in recent historic time and space, not only like us in his humanity—but, as the Person Paul met on the Damascus road, a risen, transcendent Person whose life, death, resurrection, and ascension reversed the catastrophe of our sin and fallenness (1 Cor. 15:22).

In a very real sense, the name change from Saul to Paul was more than a conversion—it was an awakening: "something like scales fell from his eyes, and his sight was restored" (Acts 9:18). It was a regeneration. Paul was given a pure, unadulterated gift that he could neither earn nor deserve. Now he could see where the Law had been pointing all along—to a Person. This is why he would later write: "we proclaim Christ crucified, a stumbling block to Jews and foolishness to Gentiles, but to those who are the called, both Jews and Greeks, Christ the power of God and the wisdom of God" (1 Cor. 1:23–24). Scandalous to those bound by Jewish law and tradition and madness for those absorbed in Greek elite culture and Western philosophical worldviews. But for those who could believe that Jesus was the Christ of God (in Greek, *Christ* means "anointed One"), by the grace of God, he became their salvation.[14]

The first Christians did not preach a system or even a religion. They proclaimed a *Person*. For Islam the Word became a *book*

---

13. *Dikaioun*, "to be made righteous" (or in the phrase made famous by the Protestant Reformation in the sixteenth century, "to be justified"), denotes that there is a grace that comes from outside of ourselves.

14. *Strong's Concordance of the New Testament* indicates that *charis*, "grace," appears at least eighty-eight times in Paul's letters to first-century churches.

(Qu'ran); for Christianity the Word became *flesh* (John 1:14).[15] A human being. The Eternal, One God, became a Person. Incarnation. The first Christians did not give up their lives for a theory, a principle, or a life force. It was for and because of a Person—a real Person who was really crucified and buried, who was really raised from the dead as the firstfruits of the new creation, who really ascended into heaven, and who is really coming back again.

I know of no one who describes this more articulately than Dietrich Bonhoeffer: "With an abstract idea it is possible to enter into a relation of formal knowledge, to become enthusiastic about it, and perhaps even to put it into practice; but it can never be followed in personal obedience. Christianity without the living Christ is inevitably Christianity without discipleship, and Christianity without discipleship is always Christianity without Christ."[16]

So the journey of grace is not about following a system, a book, a *Manual*, a denomination, or a tradition. We follow, worship, and serve Jesus Christ. Grace is the result of all the benefits of the life, ministry, death, resurrection, and ascension of the personal Jesus, who is now Christ and Lord.

A Christocentric (Jesus-centered) account of grace is not to neglect a more robust Trinitarian theology of grace (God as Creator and Father; the power of the Holy Spirit in a believer's life). Understanding grace as a Person is to remember that whatever we come to personally know of God is revealed most clearly in the life, teaching, and experience of the Person God has chosen to make himself known. The goal of all Christian discipleship is to shape the recipients of

---

15. I am indebted to Dany Gomis, Church of the Nazarene Regional Director for Africa, for this important distinction.

16. Dietrich Bonhoeffer, *The Cost of Discipleship* (New York: Macmillan Company, 1949), 63–64.

grace into the image and likeness of Jesus Christ. Grace is not some-thing—grace is some*one*.

This affirmation leads us to the second reason that grace is personal: grace comes to every person according to his or her particular need or capacity to receive it. Each person uniquely receives and appropriates grace.

I have many friends, but I relate to them in different ways because each one is unique. I have three children, and while I love them all an equal amount, I cannot treat them all the same way. They are all different, so my parenting approach must adapt for each one. This is the loving way to be a friend and to be a parent.

Likewise, grace is appropriated and received uniquely by every person because we experience grace in a personal relationship with the triune God, given to us from the Father, extended through Jesus Christ, and empowered by the Holy Spirit. Grace is personal because it comes to us in a Person, personalized according to our needs. As God gives more of himself to us, more grace is given.

Grace Is Costly

Dietrich Bonhoeffer reminds us that, although grace is free, it doesn't come without a cost. In a piercing paragraph from his most well-known book, *The Cost of Discipleship*, Bonhoeffer highlights the difference between cheap grace and costly grace as a lack of demand for or expectation of real discipleship: "Cheap grace is grace without discipleship, grace without the cross, grace without Jesus Christ, living and incarnate."[17]

Further, Bonhoeffer bluntly states that cheap grace is the "deadly enemy of our church," "the bitterest foe of discipleship," and "has been the ruin of more Christians than any commandment of works."[18]

17. Bonhoeffer, *The Cost of Discipleship*, 47–48.
18. Bonhoeffer, *The Cost of Discipleship*, 45, 55, 59.

One can say they are justified by grace alone as a gift from God, but the fruit of a justified life is the one who has left all and followed Christ.[19] And the reason, Bonhoeffer rightly points out, is that when one hears the call of Jesus to follow him, the response of disciples is first an act of obedience before it is a doctrinal confession of faith (Mark 2:14).[20]

Bonhoeffer goes on to describe how grace is costly and why a complete and fully surrendered discipleship is the only appropriate response:

> Grace is *costly* because it calls us to follow, and it is *grace* because it calls us to follow *Jesus Christ*. It is costly because it costs a man his life, and it is grace because it gives a man the only true life. It is costly because it condemns sin and grace because it justifies the sinner. Above all, it is costly because it cost God the life of his Son: 'ye were bought at a price,' and what cost God much cannot be cheap for us. Above all, it is grace because God did not reckon his Son too dear a price to pay for our life, but delivered him up for us. Costly grace is the Incarnation of God.[21]

The life of discipleship is a journey of grace. It begins with grace, is empowered by grace, and is infused with grace from start to finish. There is no true discipleship unless we follow and obey the way of Jesus. The grace of God can be received as a free gift, but it cannot remain apart from the demands of discipleship.

Grace Is Amazing

Philip Yancey recounts a scene from the movie *The Last Emperor*, of the young boy anointed as the last emperor of China. He lives a life of luxury with many servants at his command.

---

19. Bonhoeffer, *The Cost of Discipleship*, 55.
20. Bonhoeffer, *The Cost of Discipleship*, 61.
21. Bonhoeffer, *The Cost of Discipleship*, 47–48.

"What happens when you do wrong?" his brother asks.

"When I do wrong, someone else is punished," the boy emperor replies. To demonstrate, the boy emperor breaks a precious artifact, and one of the servants is beaten for the transgression.[22]

This was the ancient custom of kings and emperors. It was neither just nor merciful. Then someone arrived from another world. He was a King who brought new meaning to the concept of authority. He reversed the old order and inaugurated a new kingdom. When his servants fall into sin, this King takes their just due. Yancey reflects, "Grace is free only because the giver himself has borne the cost."[23]

This is not justice or mercy—this is grace. Costly grace. Perhaps this is why we still love to sing Newton's song. Grace is amazing.

So how does the extravagant grace of God play out in our daily lives? It is one thing to know what grace means. It is great to know that God loves us like that, but what does grace look like when I see it? What does grace do when I experience it? What difference does grace make in my everyday life?

Grace is experienced in multifaceted, nuanced, and diverse ways. The rest of this book will explore the manifold expressions of the journey of grace.

---

22. Yancey, *What's So Amazing about Grace?*, 67.
23. Yancey, *What's So Amazing About Grace?*, 67.

△
THE WAY

*Through seeking (or prevenient) grace,
God goes before us to make a way and
draw us into relationship.*

▲

2
SEEKING GRACE*
For the Son of Man came to seek out and to save the lost.
—Luke 19:10

Discipleship is akin to a long obedience in the same direction with Jesus as our guide and companion.[1] We call this a journey of grace. The journey of grace is always dynamic because it is relational to the core. Walking by faith is more adventure than drudgery, more delight than duty, with every step of the discipleship journey immersed in the grace of God. We experience God's grace in different ways through various seasons of our lives. While these facets of grace are not always sequential (following in a specific order), they are differentiated according to the varying purposes they fulfill in our discipleship journeys.[2]

---

1. The phrase "a long obedience in the same direction" is borrowed from a book on discipleship authored by pastor-theologian Eugene Peterson. Eugene Peterson, *A Long Obedience in the Same Direction: Discipleship in an Instant Society* (Downers Grove, IL: InterVarsity Press, 1980).

2. While grace may not be experienced sequentially, theologians do refer to an order of salvation (*ordo salutis*). Nonetheless, Diane LeClerc makes the important point:

---

*Portions of this chapter are included and adapted from the author's chapter entitled "The Grace That Goes Before: Prevenient Grace in the Wesleyan Spirit," by David A. Busic, in *Wesleyan Foundations for Evangelism*, ed. by Al Truesdale (Kansas City, MO: The Foundry Publishing, 2020). Used by permission.

There are at least five scriptural motifs that portray how we experience the grace of God. That is not to say there are different classifications of grace, as if grace could be dissected into different categorical measurements or types.[3] As Jack Jackson points out, "God's grace is singular,"[4] or, from John Wesley, God's grace is simply "the love of God."[5] To avoid this tendency to classify various types of grace, Wesley chose to focus on the experiential nature of grace: "Depending on their stage of discipleship, people experience God's grace differently. Those in the state of nature (pre-Christian) experience grace preveniently; once awakened, they experience grace in a convincing and justifying manner; and then, finally, once they are justified, they experience grace working to sanctify their minds and hearts."[6] Jackson's description here of Wesley's theology is beautifully written, logical yet flexible, distinguishing between grace as a thing and grace as a relational journey that includes life circumstances and experiences, divine appointments, and providential timing. Grace is a Person, and is extended in personal ways.

"Since this is often considered a series of steps in the Christian life, some scholars prefer *via salutis*, or way of salvation, to emphasize the fluidity of one stage to another." Diane LeClerc, *Discovering Christian Holiness: The Heart of Wesleyan-Holiness Theology* (Kansas City, MO: Beacon Hill Press of Kansas City, 2010), 315.

3. This was a major point in the last chapter. Grace is not a thing—grace is a person and personal. Tom Noble suggests the tendency of treating grace as an objective force or substance came from medieval Augustinianism. Different types of grace emerged that could be infused into Christians. The tendency expanded in seventeenth-century Protestant scholasticism. "That scholastic model of grace brings its own problems, particularly a tendency to depersonalize the action of God, replacing the personal action of the Spirit with this impersonal substance called 'grace.'" T. A. Noble, *Holy Trinity: Holy People: The Theology of Christian Perfecting* (Eugene, OR: Cascade Books, 2013), 100.

4. Jack Jackson, *Offering Christ: John Wesley's Evangelistic Vision* (Nashville: Kingswood Books, 2017), 53.

5. John Wesley, Sermon 110, "Free Grace," *Sermons III: 71–114*, vol. 3 in *The Bicentennial Edition of the Works of John Wesley* (Nashville: Abingdon Press, 1986), 3:544, par. 1.

6. Jackson, *Offering Christ*, 53.

With that in mind, I offer the following motifs to help us better understand how we often experience God's love on the journey of grace, recognizing that these are not different *kinds* of grace but that these are the different ways that we may experience God as Grace Personified over the course of our lives.[7]

- Seeking Grace
- Saving Grace
- Sanctifying Grace
- Sustaining Grace
- Sufficient Grace

In the chapters that follow, we will examine each of these motifs in detail biblically, theologically, and experientially. We begin here with seeking grace.

The Grace That Goes Before

The grace of God does not begin at the moment of our salvation. It precedes even the awareness of our need for God. We do not naturally seek God; instead, God seeks us. The theological term for this action by which God seeks to draw us nearer to himself is *prevenient grace*. Prevenient grace simply means that God comes to us before we come to God. God's grace seeks us out and comes to where we are.

Christians often begin conversion testimonies with pronouncements that they "came to Christ" at such and such a place or at a certain age. These are genuine attempts to recount a specific time and place when they had an encounter with God and experienced new

---

7. Following William Greathouse and H. Ray Dunning's understanding of "salvation" as a theological term having broad connotations: "[Salvation] encompasses the whole work of God directed toward restoring man to his lost estate. Beginning with initial salvation, it includes all aspects of that restoration up to and including final salvation or 'glorification.'" William M. Greathouse and H. Ray Dunning, *An Introduction to Wesleyan Theology* (Kansas City, MO: Beacon Hill Press of Kansas City, 1982), 75. Further, Greathouse and Dunning explain that salvation is not located in one singular event or experience: "The New Testament speaks of salvation in three tenses: past (have been), present (are being), and future (will be)."

birth in Christ, but the wording "came to Christ" is not exactly accurate because no one ever *comes* to Jesus Christ. *Jesus Christ comes to us.*

In a very important letter written to the first gentile Christians, the apostle Paul says, "You were dead through the trespasses and sins in which you once lived, following the course of this world. But God, who is rich in mercy, out of the great love with which he loved us even when we were dead through our trespasses, made us alive together with Christ—by grace you have been saved" (Eph. 2:1–2a, 4–5). Take special note of a word repeated for special emphasis: *dead.* Paul takes this very seriously. He does not say we were "sick" in our sins or "stuck" in our sins. No, we were *dead* in our sins.

According to the Bible, there are three kinds of death: physical, spiritual, and eternal. Paul is describing spiritual death. We were living and breathing and going through the motions of life but were spiritually dead because of sin. A person can be physically alive and walking around, but on the inside, they cannot respond to spiritual things because they have no spiritual sensation. That is why someone who is spiritually dead doesn't connect with spiritual truth. It is no more real to them than a sense of smell would be to a dead person. Dead people are non-responsive, disconnected from others, and unaware of their surroundings.

Paul says we were all in this zombie-like condition of the walking dead. Since the dead cannot respond to outside stimuli, no spiritually dead person can "come to Christ" by his or her own strength. Help must come from the outside. So, according to Paul and other scriptural witnesses, God intervenes in our desperate situation and does something for us that we cannot do for ourselves: God comes to where we are. By the power of the Holy Spirit, God moves toward us and awakens our spiritual sensitivities. This reality leads to a profound thought: Even our capacity to say no to the promptings of God are made possible only because God's prevenient grace has already encountered us. We are only free to respond to God because God has freed our spiritual consciousness to do so. A movement of grace upon us precedes any response to God.

Sleeping Beauty is a famous fairy tale about a princess who is under the enchanted spell of a wicked queen. The princess remains in a perpetual state of sleep, and the only way she can be awakened is if her prince comes and kisses her. This kiss will arouse her from her comatose state and rescue her from her hopeless condition. Though it is only a fairy tale, it is symbolic of how prevenient grace works. The Bible says that every human soul is in a kind of spiritual death sleep, and that we are incapable of bringing ourselves to spiritual consciousness. Then the Prince comes and kisses us, the spell is broken, and we are awakened to new realities previously unknown. Just as the lovesick father of Luke 15 runs to his disgraced son at the end of the road, so this kiss represents prevenient grace. Read these words from the moving parable again through the lens of prevenient grace: "But while he was still *far off*, his father saw him and was filled with compassion; he ran and put his arms around him and *kissed* him, 'for this son of mine was dead and is alive again; he was lost and is found!' And they began to celebrate" (Luke 15:20b, 24, emphases added).

John Wesley and Prevenient Grace

Our theological forefather John Wesley had much to say about prevenient grace. While he did not believe that actual discipleship begins until after conversion, he maintained that God's grace works in advance, stirring up in people the desire to begin seeking God, the desire of which marks the beginning of awakening.[8] We seek God only because God is first seeking us.

---

8. Jackson, *Offering Christ*, 43–44. See also Randy Maddox, *Responsible Grace: John Wesley's Practical Theology* (Nashville: Kingswood, 1994), 81.

John Wesley was not the first to embrace the idea of the power of prevenient grace extended to all people, but he certainly added his own distinction in the order of salvation.[9] Sometimes referring to it as "preventing grace," Wesley believed that from birth, God's grace is active in all persons, seeking to draw them to eternal life in Jesus Christ. This is true even if they have never heard the gospel proclaimed. God's prior presence and action through the Holy Spirit is the grace that "goes before" hearing the good news, spiritual awakening, and conversion.

No person is a stranger to God's grace, and everyone is the object of the Spirit of Jesus's wooing. As fallen human beings, "dead in our transgressions and sins" (Eph. 2:1, NIV), we are rendered incapable of coming to God in our own strength. Therefore, God is always the first one on the scene of all awakening, conversion, and life transformation. We call the initial activity of the Holy Spirit "prevenient" because it always precedes our response. One may come to *faith* in Jesus Christ, but no one ever "comes to Christ" unless God first draws and enables them. Jesus told his disciples that would be the work of the Holy Spirit (John 16:5–15; see also John 6:44).

As Lovett Weems puts it, "God seeks us before we ever seek God. The initiative of salvation is with God from the beginning. Before we ever take a step, God is there."[10] Grace is not irresistible, but no person is left without the invitation of a personal relationship with God. What this means for those in the Wesleyan-Holiness tradition is that, when sharing the gospel with someone, we never encounter a morally neutral context. There is no person we meet who has not been affected by prevenient grace. Certainly, some will be more re-

---

9. In the Catholic tradition, "actual grace" is divided into two parts: "operating prevenient grace" and "cooperating subsequent grace."

10. Lovett H. Weems, Jr., *John Wesley's Message Today* (Nashville: Abingdon Press, 1991), 23.

sistant or responsive than others, but we can rest assured that God has been faithfully active in their lives long before we arrive on the scene. The Prince has preceded our entry onto their life stage.

God's offer of salvation is not coercive. By its nature, reciprocal love (the basis of true relationship) requires the freedom to accept or reject offered love. Nevertheless, prevenient grace both precedes our response *and* enables our response. This is the order of redemption and the beginning of discipleship. God initiates; we respond. Grace always goes first.

Working Out What God Is Working In

The entire New Testament bears witness, and the apostle Paul's writings especially emphasize that "when a person has come to faith in Jesus as the risen Lord, that event is itself a sign of the Spirit's work through the gospel, and that, if the Spirit has begun that 'good work' of which that faith is the first fruit, you can trust that the Spirit will finish the job."[11] However, this assurance does not negate the importance of human participation. Relationship entails cooperation.

Paul emphasizes who begins and finishes the journey of grace: "I am confident of this, that the one who *began* a good work among you will bring it to completion by the day of Jesus Christ" (Phil. 1:6, emphasis added).[12] Moreover, the disciple (and church) of Jesus must "work out your own salvation with fear and trembling; for it is God who is at work in you, enabling you both to will and to work for his good pleasure" (2:12b–13).[13] We must, by grace, work *out* in the world what God is working *in* us. Helpful biblical examples abound.

---

11. N. T. Wright, *Paul: A Biography* (San Francisco: HarperOne, 2018), 96.

12. Notice that God is both the initiator and enabler of the journey of grace.

13. I add the church here because the word "you" is in the plural. One could translate this in the southern American dialect of "y'all" or "you all" as a way of emphasizing the corporate nature of discipleship.

God came to Abraham in a place called Ur of the Chaldeans (now called Iran). God initiated the call: "I will make of you a great nation, and I will bless you, and make your name great, so that you will be a blessing" (Gen. 12:2). Who went first? God did. Who began the good work in Abraham? God did. But Abraham had to respond in obedience to work *out* in the world what God was working *in* him.

God came to Jacob in a dream revealing a stairway to heaven (Gen. 28:10–22) and later wrestled with Jacob at the Jabbok River (32:22–32). Who went first? God did. Who began the good work in Jacob? God did. But Jacob had to work *out* what God was working *in* him.

Moses was a hundred miles from nowhere. God came to him through a burning bush and called him to rescue his people from slavery in Egypt (Exod. 3:1–4:17). Who went first? God did. Who began the good work in Moses? God did. But Moses had to work *out* what God was working *in* him.

The living Christ appeared to Saul (or assaulted him) on the road to Damascus (Acts 9:1–19). Saul was not searching for God. He was on a mission to persecute Christians. Who went first? God did. Who began the good work in Saul—who soon became Paul, missionary to the gentiles? God did. But, as Paul would later say in his letter to the Philippian church, he had to work *out* what God was working *in* him.

The eunuch from Africa on a desert road in Judea (Acts 8), Cornelius through a vision at three in the afternoon (Acts 10), Lydia by a riverside (Acts 16): what do they all share in common? These and many other stories like them show people responding in faith to the God who first came to them. All of them were working *out* what God was working *in* them.

There is a consistent pattern of God acting with prevenient grace and people responding in faith. British missiologist Lesslie Newbigin famously said, "Faith is the hand that grasps the finished work of Christ and makes it my own." It does not remove the need for a response, but prevenient grace always comes first. Even Augustine, who was a steadfast proponent of predestination, affirmed: "He that made us without ourselves, will not save us without ourselves."[14]

Providence and Prevenience

There is a difference between providential grace and prevenient grace. Providence is how God provides for the sustenance and provision of his creation, including human beings.[15] God "provides" or "sees to" (Gen. 22:8, 14) what is needed to sustain the world and to provide for individual persons.

How God's providence intersects every person's life is profoundly mysterious. When and where and into what family one is born is a question of providence. Why one person is born into a Hindu family in India in 1765, while another person is born into a Christian family in Mozambique in 2020, are matters of providence. God's providence carries varying degrees of spiritual responsibility. One who is given the opportunity to hear the gospel throughout their life will be judged differently than one who has never heard the name of Jesus. Jesus's parable of the faithful and wise servant is about more than material possessions—it involves stewardship of God's grace. "From everyone to whom much has been given, much will be required; and from the one to whom much has been entrusted, even more will be demanded" (Luke 12:48). Not all are given equal opportunity and the same ground on which to stand. Some are given more, and some are given less. With the gift of "more" comes an increased requirement for response. These are matters of divine providence.

---

14. Quoted in John Wesley, *The Works of the Rev. John Wesley* (Kansas City, MO: Nazarene Publishing House, n.d.; and Grand Rapids: Zondervan Publishing House, 1958, concurrent editions), VI, 513.

15. The word "providence" comes from two Latin words: *pro*, which means "forward" or "on behalf of;" and, *videre*, which means "to see." Providence is sometimes distinguished into two categories: "general providence," God's care for the universe; and "special providence," God's intervention in the lives of people.

If providence is where God places us, prevenience describes the multifaceted ways that God meets us. Everyone receives the same grace that goes before salvation. But opportunities for response differ. God persistently and patiently extends himself to everyone. This belief distinguishes Christianity from other world religions that teach that God will respond if humans first move toward God. Christianity reverses the order: God always acts first, thereby enabling response.

God initiates the good work of grace and peace. Redemption and new creation always begin with God's initiative. Nothing reveals this more than the conviction that the Father sent Jesus Christ into the world. God always acts first. The Holy Spirit of God awakens persons to their need for salvation, convicts them of sin, and applies the atonement of Christ as they respond in faith.

For John Wesley, spiritual awakening is more than mere conscience: "There is no man, unless he has quenched the Spirit, that is wholly devoid of the grace of God. No man living is entirely destitute of what is vulgarly called natural conscience. Every man has some measure of that light . . . which lightens every man that comes into the world. And every one . . . feels more or less uneasy when he acts contrary to the light of his own conscience. So that no man sins because he has not grace, but because he does not use the grace which he hath."[16] An uneasy conscience, increasing awareness of right and wrong, and awakening spiritual awareness are God's gracious gifts to everyone. This confidence has important implications for evangelism in the Wesleyan spirit.

Prevenient Grace and Evangelism

I once met with a group of Christian pastors who live in a place where it is difficult to be a follower of Christ. It is not illegal to be a Christian, but there are strict national laws against proselytizing.

---

16. Wesley, *Works*, VI, 512.

Overt Christian evangelism is severely punished with imprisonment and even death. I asked the pastors how evangelism happens in such a hostile and dangerous environment. After a few moments of silence, a pastor answered, "Dreams." I did not understand, so I asked him to explain. "Not dozens, but hundreds of our neighbors are having dreams in the night. The risen Christ appears to them in all of his beauty and majesty. When they awake, they come asking questions. 'Tell us about this man who comes to us in the night.' When they ask, it is our obligation to answer. We are not evangelizing. We are merely bearing witness to their own experiences. Many of them are committing their lives to Christ in that way."

In places where the church is facing closed doors, the Spirit of God is going ahead of us. The prevenient grace of God knows no boundaries or barriers. The love of God relentlessly reaches even the most difficult, resistant, and hostile persons. They may never respond in obedient faith, but they cannot escape the pervasive presence of the God who will not stop loving and drawing them.

That has been the repeated story of the *Jesus Film*. This movie dramatically recounts the life of Christ. It has been an effective instrument of grace in the lives of multiplied thousands around the world. It has been shown to people in remote areas where the name of Jesus has never been spoken. It has been told that the chief of a tribe stood in the middle of a showing and said, "Stop! We know this man! He appeared to our ancestors many years ago and revealed this story of salvation. He said that one day someone would come to tell us his name. And now we know his name is Jesus." While this is only one example of other similar stories, it shows that the Spirit of God is far ahead of the church, as is always the case. The Holy Spirit had been cultivating the soil of their hearts to receive the gospel. Prevenient grace intersected with God's providential design long before the church arrived to proclaim the good news. As a result, often an entire tribe puts its faith in Christ.

Christian evangelism is neither a solo act nor a solitary moment. It happens in relational interactions prompted by the Holy Spirit, who always graciously goes before. No Christian can look in life's rearview mirror and fail to see the marvelous ways God has acted to awaken and bring them to repentance and faith in Christ Jesus.

My father became a Christian as a young teenager through Nazarene foster parents. I became a Christian through the example of Christian parents and a group of men who faithfully met every Wednesday morning to pray specifically for my salvation. Your journey of grace is unique to you. What remains the same for everyone is that God always goes before.

My friend Stephane was an atheist attending a university in Germany where he was studying robotic science. His atheist uncle told him about a movie called *The Mission*. He encouraged him to watch the movie because of its "impeccable acting and beautiful landscapes." The movie is set in the eighteenth century, in the northeastern jungles of Argentina. A Spanish Jesuit mission has been established to reach the Guarani indigenous tribes for Christ.

Stephane rented the movie. He was especially moved by a scene where a slave trader and mercenary named Rodrigo Mendoza climbs a steep mountain waterfall. Strapped to his back are the tools of his trade—his armor and his swords. He is doing penance for his many sins. As Mendoza reaches the top of the precipice, a warrior from the tribe Mendoza kidnapped and sold into slavery jumped toward him, holding a knife as if to cut Mendoza's throat. After hesitating a moment, the tribesman cuts the rope from Mendoza's shoulders and sends the heavy pack tumbling to the bottom of the waterfall. Mendoza is suddenly aware that something has changed this young warrior from a having thirst for vengeance to being willing to show mercy. Exhausted and covered with mud, Mendoza falls to the ground. He begins to weep uncontrollably, not from tears of remorse but from joy born of inner peace. He is given sanctuary in the village and welcomed into their community. Eventually Mendoza takes the vows of a Jesuit priest.

Later, Mendoza is given a book from which he reads a passage on the meaning of love. Stephane did not know the source of the words, but he said they were the most poetic and beautiful words he had ever heard. They so captured him that he watched the scene repeatedly and meticulously. He wrote the words down so as not to forget them. He then went to a library to research the poem's source. To his surprise, the words were from the Bible. He repeatedly read 1 Corinthians 13—"the love chapter."

Not long afterward, Stephane became romantically interested in a fellow college student. One night she invited Stephane to what she called a "club." It turned out to be a Bible study. Stephane learned the Lord's Prayer. As a scientist, he believed in experimentation to determine logical outcomes. Stephane found that, every time he prayed the Lord's Prayer before going to bed, he rested peacefully. Soon he began to pray before bed each night. He was being awakened by a pursuing love and a grace going ahead.

The missionary God began to answer the prayers of a young atheist. He discovered the splendor of God's love through a movie containing "impeccable acting and beautiful landscapes." Stephane responded to the grace that goes before. He confessed his faith in Christ and began to work *out* in the world what God was working *in* him. Stephane is now a missionary in the Church of the Nazarene. Such is the prevenient grace of God that leads to repentance and transformation.

Belief in the power of prevenient grace makes it impossible to despair of anyone who has not yet become a Christian. We must never give up hope for anyone because God does not. The confidence of evangelists rests neither in themselves nor in the ability of those hearing the gospel. Rather, our absolute confidence is that God's love is for everyone. It is extravagant (Eph. 1:7), relentless, and unchangeable. It is sufficient to complete what God begins. Divine appointments await!

How far will God go to reach one person? I have come to appreciate the lyrics of Cory Asbury's 2017 song "Reckless Love," about the seeking grace of God. The song talks about God's grace in the singer's life "before I spoke a word" and "before I took a breath." It describes the "overwhelming, never-ending, reckless love of God" that "chases me down, fights 'til I'm found, leaves the ninety-nine." The chorus goes like this:

There's no shadow you won't light up

Mountain you won't climb up

Coming after me

There's no wall you won't kick down

Lie you won't tear down

Coming after me.[17]

Overwhelming. Never-ending. *That* is how far God will go to reach one person.

---

17. Some have expressed concern over use of the word "reckless." If it means careless, it is problematic. If it means bold, surprising, and extravagant, it is getting closer to describing the love of God.

△□
THE TRUTH

Through saving grace, Jesus rescues us from sin and leads us into the truth that makes us free.

3
SAVING GRACE

*For the wages of sin is death, but the free gift of God
is eternal life in Christ Jesus our Lord.*
—Romans 6:23

A sports reporter once asked renowned championship golfer Jack Nicklaus to identify the most common problem for amateur golfers. Expecting him to say something about a lack of practice or the inability to putt consistently well, I was surprised when Nicklaus instead responded, "Overconfidence." Thinking they are better than they really are or can do more than they really can. *I think I can hit this shot between those two trees. I can probably drive the ball over the water.* That is overconfidence.

People do it all the time. They vastly overrate their abilities and underrate their limitations. But nowhere does the problem of overrating happen more frequently than in the spiritual realm. We vastly overrate our spiritual strength and underrate our spiritual weakness.

Moralism

This tendency for spiritually overrating oneself is called moralism. Moralism is the self-righteous belief that all is well spiritually because one leads a decent moral life and has improved their behavior. Said in another way, a moralist is someone who believes they are saved by the good they do and the bad they avoid.

Moralists all say similar things: "I'm no Mother Teresa, but I'm not all that bad either. I make an honest living. I pay back my debts. I don't cheat on my spouse. I vote responsibly. I give a little money to charity. I'm not a spiritual fanatic, but I'm not all that bad either." In other words, moralists follow the line of thinking that tells them God will take into account on Judgment Day the fact that they do more good than bad, especially compared to "other" people (serial killers, rapists, drug dealers, etc.) who are much worse. Moralism is rampant in our world today.

In 2004, the Gallup organization conducted a poll to find out what Americans believe about heaven. What really caught my attention is the number of people who believe they are going to heaven: 77 percent of those who said they believe in heaven ranked their chances of getting there as "good" or "excellent." But, according to those surveyed, only six out of ten of their friends are going to heaven. Of most interest to me, especially pertaining to a moralistic viewpoint, is that many of the people in the survey affirmed the belief that "there is a heaven where people who have *led good lives* are eternally rewarded."[1] I emphasize "led good lives" to make the point that most people believe they are going to heaven when they die because of their "good lives" and "moral behavior."

Diana, Princess of Wales, died in 1997. It was a tragic loss to many around the world. Media attention and public mourning were extensive due to her international popularity. I remember listening to people talk about how comforting it was to know that Diana was now

---

1. Albert L. Winseman, "Eternal Destinations: Americans Believe in Heaven, Hell," May 25, 2004, https://news.gallup.com/poll/11770/eternal-destinations-americans-believe-heaven-hell.aspx.

in heaven and that she was an angel looking out for them and that heaven was a better place for her than this world. I am not suggesting that Diana is not in heaven, but I wonder about the reasoning behind so many people saying she is there. From all I can observe she was a kind, compassionate person who used her considerable influence for good. She worked with the poor, was an advocate for AIDS patients, and her activism helped raise awareness for children and youth. These are all wonderful things to be known for, but do they save us? Can *being* good or *doing* good lead to salvation, heaven, and eternal reward?

We live in an age of diverse opinions relative to these questions. Many people maintain that God grades on the curve and that a little goodness goes a long way. If we can just pile up more things in the "good" column than the "bad" column, somehow the scale will be weighted in our favor, and our *pretty good lives* and *honest efforts* will more than compensate the difference. That is moralism and good-works righteousness.

God's Word is clear on this point, however: we are not saved by our efforts; we are not saved by our goodness; we are not saved by our intentions. We are saved by grace, and grace comes from outside ourselves. Saving grace comes from God in the person of Jesus Christ.

The Atonement

The cross is perhaps the most widely known and recognized symbol in the world today. When we see the cross, we are reminded of Jesus's life and death by crucifixion. Crucifixion was the most horrendous and torturous form of execution ever invented by humankind. For that reason, a person in the first century would find it odd to see modern people wearing a cross on a chain around their necks. If we today saw a person wearing an icon of an electric chair on a necklace, we would think that was odd because it represents a means of criminal punishment and death. That is what the cross was for folks in the first century. It was disgraceful and distasteful. It was the fate of hardened criminals and insurrectionists. Crucifixion was so completely appalling that a word was created to explain it. Our English word "excruciating" literally means "from the cross."

Death by crucifixion was a slow, agonizing, public way to die. There was no obscurity. Those being crucified were often mocked and jeered. The watching crowd threw stones and laughed as those hanging on a cross slowly descended into a state of deep, labored breathing and gasping for breath. They ultimately died of asphyxiation because, as they hung suspended, their lungs had difficulty continuing to operate. It could sometimes take several days for someone finally to die, and then those who were crucified were not given a humane burial. Instead, they were often left for the birds to pick away their flesh. After enough time had passed for the dead to serve as an example for any who would defy the Roman Empire, whatever was left of the corpse was taken down and thrown into the city garbage dump.

Let us not forget that Jesus was crucified on a criminal's cross— which leads me to say that which even now seems highly peculiar: Christians declare this to be *good news*. In fact, we say it is the best news we have ever heard. The word the Bible chooses to express this good news is "gospel." The cross is our gospel—our good news.

In the shortest summary of the gospel in the New Testament, the apostle Paul declared, "For I handed on to you as of first importance what I in turn had received: that *Christ died. . .*" (1 Cor. 15:3a, emphasis added). Now, all by itself, that is not good news, but then Paul gives a theological meaning to Christ's death through a profoundly important preposition, "for," to move us from a tragic fact of history to its remarkable relevance for our journey of grace: "that Christ died *for* our sins in accordance with the scriptures" (v. 3b, emphasis added). When the "for" is added it becomes good news—the best news we have ever heard.

Theologically, Scripture calls this the atonement. Atonement can also be broken down to mean "at-one-ment" (meaning we are *at one* with God through Christ's atonement). Atonement was made through the cross of Jesus Christ. The doctrine of the atonement begins in the Old Testament. The Day of Atonement, also called Yom Kippur, was the holiest day in ancient Judaism.[2] It was designated as a day of repentance and forgiveness.

Picture it in your mind. Imagine thousands of worshipers coming together to begin the year by having their sins atoned for and to be reminded of God's mercy. On that day the high priest, representing all the people, brought two goats forward. One goat was sacrificed as a sin offering to make atonement for the Holy of Holies and the altar of God. Blood was shed, and the animal died. Romans 6:23 tells us that "the wages of sin is death," and Hebrews 9:22 reminds us that "without the shedding of blood there is no forgiveness of sins."

The first goat died according to the law. The second goat, however, was kept alive and was called the scapegoat. The high priest laid his hands on the head of the scapegoat and confessed over it all the wickedness and sins of the Israelites. Symbolically, these sins were placed on the goat's head, and then it was driven into the wilderness to a solitary place where the people's sins could be carried far away and out of sight.[3]

That ritual went on year after year, decade after decade (see Hebrews 10:3–4). Blood flowed. Thousands of animals were sacrificed in an endless cycle of atonement to deal with the sins of the people. That is the background context in which Jesus lived and ministered. Before we consider how Jesus's death on the cross made atonement for all sin,

---

2. *Yom* = "day;" *Kippur* = "to atone; cleanse."

3. Tradition tells us that the man appointed to the task of releasing the scapegoat was a gentile who had no connection with the people of Israel.

making saving grace a possibility, let us first consider two fundamental questions: What is sin? And why do we need atonement for sin?

What Is Sin?

First, sin is rebellion. Perhaps the most recognizable definition of sin comes from John Wesley: "a voluntary transgression of a known law of God."[4] Sin is something that is known and willful—something we know is wrong but we do it anyway because we can. It is willful disobedience.

When 1 John 3:4 tells us that "everyone who commits sin is guilty of lawlessness; sin is lawlessness," it is not referring only to the legalistic sense, as in "you broke the law." It has to do with the attitude behind law-breaking. An analogy may help us understand. It is one thing to drive over the speed limit because you didn't know what the speed limit was. You might still be technically breaking the law, but you are not acting lawlessly. That is very different from a person who says, "Forget these stupid speed limit regulations. They are just there to try to control me. I'll do what I want because I'm in charge of my life." Lawlessness is the attitude of rebellion behind law-breaking—a rebellious spirit.

When my youngest daughter was little, she didn't like having to answer to her older sister and brother when Mom and Dad were not around. When my wife and I left them alone together, our youngest defiantly raised her squeaky little voice and said to her siblings, "You're not the boss of me!" Though said with the innocence of a small child, it is the heart attitude of sin: self-sovereignty. Sin as rebellion is shaking our tiny little fists in the face of almighty God and shouting: "You're not the boss of me! I'll do it my way because I can! Nobody but me, not even God, is going to be in charge of my life."

---

4. John Wesley, *The Works of John Wesley*, vol. 12 (Kansas City, MO: Beacon Hill Press of Kansas City, 1978), 394. See also James 4:17.

It is refusing to accept our role as creatures with our Creator. It is a declaration of independence to be our own god.

This attitude of self-sovereignty is not surprising to the writers of Scripture. "All we like sheep have gone astray; we have all turned to our own way, and the LORD has laid on him the iniquity of us all" (Isa. 53:6). Sin is rebellion.

Second, sin is also enslavement. It is more than self-sovereignty and choosing to do our own thing and walk our own path. *Hamartia* is a Greek word translated as sin that derives from the verb *hamartano*, meaning "to miss the mark" or "to shoot at a target and fail to hit it."[5] Though it was first used by Aristotle, particularly referring to the tragic flaw of a main character from the ancient Greek world of theater (such as bad judgment, ignorance, lack of awareness, etc.), and also known as tragedy, early church writers and thinkers picked up on the word to describe this aspect of sin. So biblically, *hamartia* can mean an act of *commission*: "I knew I shouldn't do it, but I did it anyway" (see Rom. 6:1–2); or it can mean an act of *omission*: "I knew what I was supposed to do, but I didn't do it" (Rom. 7:19; James 4:17). Both sins of commission and omission miss the mark.

Here is how it might play out in the world of business. On one hand, I want God to bless my business, but I also want to guarantee that my business will be successful. So I begin to do some things on the sly to try and get ahead, even though I know they aren't ethical or legal. These hopes conflict and are incompatible with my actions. I cannot ask God to bless my work knowing full well that I am outside the moral will of God. That is a sin of commission. It may get me ahead for a season, but it will not have the favor of God. The reverse side of the same coin is that I want God to prosper my work, but I

5. William Barclay, *The Gospel of Matthew*, vol. 1 (Louisville, KY: Westminster John Knox Press, 1956), 253. See also H. G. Liddell, *A Lexicon: Abridged from Liddell and Scott's Greek-English Lexicon* (Oak Harbor, WA: Logos Research Systems, Inc., 1996), 41.

decide to withhold fair advantages and benefits from my employees to pad my earnings. That is a sin of omission. However, whether the sin is to know what I should *not do* and do it anyway, or to know what I *should do* and not do it, both are the same in God's eyes.

Hamartia can also mean something much deeper. More than an action we take, sin is our nature—a condition in which we find ourselves.[6] We are enmeshed in sin. Not only are we rebels by nature, but we are also not free to do otherwise. Not only do we miss the mark, but we also couldn't hit the mark if we tried. As fallen people, we are not free to do as we wish. We are captive to sin.

We often think our rebellion means that no one but us will be in charge of our lives, but what we misunderstand is that we don't get to make that choice. We *will* serve somebody or something. Either we will serve God with our whole heart, or we will be enslaved to our passions and sinful behaviors. One or the other will be our master.

Let's be honest: sin can be fun. If it were not fun, it would not be tempting. If it weren't enjoyable, it wouldn't be alluring. Perhaps we should stop telling people how much they are going to hate sin and how boring it really is. It is not a convincing argument. Sin can be fun—for a while. But eventually, the path where sin always leads is destructive. The consequences (wages) of sin are what hurt. Sin is a vicious cycle.

Partying can be fun. Where it can lead is not. Drunkenness is not fun. Hangovers are not fun. Alcoholism is not fun. Addictions are not fun. Detox centers are not fun. Car accidents are not fun. Spousal abuse is not fun. Dysfunctional families are not fun. Sin is a vicious cycle that leads to painful destruction.

---

6. Wesleyan-Holiness people understand that sin involves more than an action taken. Susanna Wesley is renowned for her statement written in a letter to her son John, June 8, 1725: "Take this rule: whatever weakens your reason, impairs the tenderness of your conscience, obscures your sense of God, or takes off your relish of spiritual things; in short, whatever increases the strength and authority of your body over your mind, that thing is sin to you, however innocent it may be in itself."

Having extramarital sex with someone can be fun. Where it leads is not. A guilty conscience is not fun. Sexually transmitted diseases are not fun. Divorce is not fun. Breaking someone's heart is not fun. Looking your children in the eye and telling them why you are leaving their mother or father is not fun. Sin is a vicious cycle that leads to painful destruction.

The remarkable story Jesus told of the prodigal son is a prime example of the cycle of sin (see Luke 15:11–24). A rebellious son decides he wants to be in charge of his own life. He tells his father he wants his inheritance in advance (the equivalent in the first century of saying he wishes his father were dead), takes the entire cache of money, and spends it all on lavish and wild living. He loves the lifestyle—for a while. Then his money disappears, and so do his friends. The son finds himself in a place he never dreamed he would be: broken, humiliated, and living in a pigpen. Sin is a vicious cycle that leads to painful destruction.

Perhaps this is what Jesus meant when he said, "Enter through the narrow gate; for the gate is wide and the road is easy that leads to destruction, and there are many who take it" (Matt. 7:13).

Here is the great struggle of our sinful nature: until our nature changes, we are going to love sin more than we love God because we are enslaved to sin—in bondage to its power.[7] No amount of good intentions or hard work, no humanistic moralism, is going to liberate us completely. Sin is enslavement.

Finally, sin is estrangement. "Estrangement" is not a word we often use, but when we do, we use it to indicate that something has gone wrong in a relationship. Sin is not just breaking a rule or vio-

---

7. Geoffrey Bromiley points out the interesting fact that the Bible often "personifies" sin to highlight the power and control sin can have over our lives. Bromiley, *Theological Dictionary of the New Testament: Abridged in One Volume* (Grand Rapids: Eerdmans, 1985), 48.

lating a law; it is also damaging a relationship. Sin separates people from God and from each other. In the first recorded act of sin, our spiritual ancestors Adam and Eve disobeyed God. When they did, they immediately knew there was a breach in their relationship with God and each other. Their eyes were opened, and they realized they were naked. That means more than a recognition that they had no clothes. They felt ashamed and vulnerable; they felt weak and alienated; they felt exposed. Up until that time, they had only known the loving fellowship of God, but at the moment of their sin they felt separation from God. They *felt* the estrangement. Their fellowship was broken, and it pressed down on their souls. They *felt* the guilt of the full weight of their sin. In self-defense, they did a very telling thing: they tried to cover their nakedness and hide from God. Have you ever tried to cover up your guilt or hide your sin from God?

God knew fellowship had been broken. And in one of the most tender accounts in all of Scripture, God called out to them, "Where are you?" (Gen. 3:9). Now, did God really not know where they were? Were they doing such a good job of hiding behind the trees that God couldn't find them? Have you ever played hide and seek with a three-year-old? Of course God knew where they were! But he wanted them to know *he* also felt the separation.

The man answered, "I heard the sound of you in the garden, and I was afraid, because I was naked; and I hid myself" (v. 10). This is the first time fear is mentioned in the Bible. Do you see what sin does? Sin brings fear and guilt and shame. Sin brings alienation, condemnation, and separation. Sin makes enemies out of friends. Sin turns intimacy into hostility. Sin breaks fellowship.

This is our predicament. Sin is rebellion. Sin is enslavement. Sin is estrangement. How are we ever going to make all that right again? What are we supposed to do with all of that sin?

Let me remind you again of the greatest news we will ever hear: "For I handed on to you as of first importance what I in turn had received: that Christ died for our sins in accordance with the scriptures, and that he was buried, and that he was raised on the third day in accordance with the scriptures" (1 Cor. 15:3–4). This is supreme, self-giving love. "God proves his love for us in that while we still were sinners Christ died for us" (Rom. 5:8). While we were still sinning, Christ died anyway. "For our sake he made him to be sin who knew no sin, so that in him we might become the righteousness of God" (2 Cor. 5:21). This is saving grace.

Protestant reformer Martin Luther is accredited with calling this "the great exchange." Our death for his life; our sin for his righteousness; our condemnation for his salvation; our failures for his success; our defeat for his victory. The atonement is the act of the Trinitarian God that breaks down all the barriers our rebellion and sin have erected between us. "In this is love, not that we loved God but that he loved us and sent his Son to be the atoning sacrifice for our sins" (1 John 4:10).

What does this mean? The atonement was in the heart of God all along. All of the lambs, all of the priests, and all of the sacrifices in the temple were pointing us, leading us, to Jesus, who has become our Great High Priest, and who shed his own blood for the forgiveness of our sins. N. T. Wright expresses it well: "Throughout the New Testament, this death is therefore seen as an act of love, both the love of Jesus himself (Gal. 2:20) and the love of the God who sent him and whose bodily self-expression he was (John 3:16; 13:1, Rom. 5:6–11; 8:31–39; 1 John 4:9–10)."[8] God the Father, sent Christ the Son, by the power of the Holy Spirit, to do for us what we could never do for ourselves.

---

8. N. T. Wright, *Evil and the Justice of God* (Downers Grove, IL: InterVarsity Press, 2006), 95.

Jesus takes our sins away—past, present, and future. God remembers them no more. "As far as the east is from the west, so far he removes our transgressions from us" (Psalm 103:12). Jesus's death on the cross breaks the power of sin in our lives. Once we were slaves to our sin, in bondage and "following the ruler of the power of the air," (Eph. 2:2) and the "god of this world" (2 Cor. 4:4). Through his death on the cross, Jesus entered into mortal combat with demonic forces and overcame them once and for all.[9] He broke the power of death, hell, and the grave. With Christ's victory on the cross we are no longer in the clutch of sin; we are in the grip of grace and potentially set free (see more on this in chapter 4 on sanctifying grace).

Because of Jesus's atonement, we have been reconciled to God. Our estrangement has been taken away. The distance between us has been closed. The chasm has been crossed. Jesus is our peace who has broken down every wall (Eph. 2:14). The veil of the temple has been torn in two (Matt. 27:51). Our guilt and shame and fear of punishment have been removed. Our friendship with God has been restored. "But now in Christ Jesus you who once were far off have been brought near by the blood of Christ" (Eph. 2:13). This is saving grace.

Do you have any idea how much God loves you? The Father has taken our sin and guilt into his own heart through the Son. Though our sins are many and grievous, not least of which is the idolatry

---

9. The belief that on the cross Jesus has won the victory over the powers of evil is referred to as the *Christus Victor* theory of atonement. N. T. Wright comments, "I am inclined to see the theme of *Christus Victor*, the victory of Jesus Christ over all the powers of evil and darkness, as the central theme in atonement theology, around which all the other varied meanings of the cross find their particular niche." Wright, *Evil and the Justice of God*, 114. Conversely, Fleming Rutledge makes a strong case that all the biblical themes of atonement work together to form a beautiful whole for understanding the depth and mystery of the cross. "The truest way to receive the gospel of Christ crucified is to cultivate a deep appreciation of the way the biblical motifs interact with each other and enlarge one another. . . . No one image can do justice to the whole; all are part of the great drama of salvation." Rutledge, *The Crucifixion: Understanding the Death of Jesus Christ* (Grand Rapids: Eerdmans, 2015), 6–7.

of our hearts to pursue other gods, our Trinitarian God redeems us, makes us a new creation, and adopts us into his family. That is why forgiveness is not a flippant matter! Anyone who says, "Of course God will forgive me—that's God's job" has never understood the deep pain associated with bearing the sin of another who has stabbed your heart. A cross has been in the heart of God from all eternity. God the Father, in his only Son, Jesus Christ, by the Spirit, has provided a way of salvation. Jesus entered fully into the Father's purpose. He willingly laid down his life for us. The Sinless One for the sinful ones. The Innocent One for the guilty ones. The spotless Lamb of God came to live the life we should have lived, and die the death we deserved to die.

The life, death, and resurrection of Jesus make all things new. There is nothing more important than this truth. It is the crux of human history and the foundation of our faith. Without Jesus, there is no forgiveness of sin, no eternal life, and no relationship with a good, holy, and loving God. You can punish yourself forever in regret for your sins. You can break your spirit trying to make your peace with God, but the only way you will experience full redemption and abiding peace is when you realize that your only hope is Jesus.

We receive the gift of saving grace by believing in God. We throw ourselves on the mercy of God and put our faith in Christ alone. We trust in his victory won on the cross, we trust that the guilt of our sin is canceled, we trust that the death grip of sin is broken, our conscience is cleansed, and we find at-one-ment with God.

There are two ways to view the atonement. You could say, "If God is love, why do we need atonement?" On the other hand, we could say, "God atoned for our sins—what love!"

How Saving Grace Works

Paul says a Christian is someone who has gone through a cataclysmic change. Ephesians 2:1–10 describes the dramatic transformation—from bondage in sin to freedom in Christ—that happens when someone believes on Christ, and so is saved. It is someone who has gone from death to life, from slavery to freedom, from condemnation to acceptance, from alienation to adoption. Now in verses 8–10 Paul tells us how we get from there to here—how we actually become a Christian. It is an organic process with three parts: we are saved by grace, which leads to faith, which produces good works. That is the equation, and the order is critical. If we get the order wrong, we get it *all* wrong.

We are saved by grace. We looked extensively at the meaning of grace in chapter 1. It is good to be reminded that grace is always the beginning. Grace is always first. Grace awakens us, changes us, and gets us into right relationship with God and each other. Many people think they are Christians because of what they have done; they suppose all they have to do is be a good person and follow the teachings of the Bible and God will bless them. That is not grace—that is moralism. There is no gospel in putting our hope in what *we* can do. Our salvation is nothing we do. It is all of what God does. Our awakening, our aliveness, is all God's doing. We are not saved by what we do for God; we are saved by what God does for us. It is a total gift.

I heard a story about some seminary students who were preparing to take a final exam. In the classroom, they spent the last few minutes cramming before the exam began. When the professor came into the classroom, he announced there would be a short review before the test. Much of the review came directly from the study guide, but there was a lot of additional material that no one had prepared for. This was an unpleasant surprise for the class. When someone asked the professor about the extra material, he explained that it was all contained in their reading and that they would be responsible for all of it. It was hard to argue with the logic.

Finally, it came time to take the test. The professor said, "Leave the exam face down on your desk until everyone has one. I will tell you when to start." When the students turned them over, to their great astonishment, every answer on the test was already filled in. Even their names were written at the top in red ink. At the bottom of the last page was written, "This is the end of the exam. All the answers on the test are correct. You will receive an A. The reason you passed the test is that the creator of the test took it for you. All the work you did in preparation did not help you get the A. You have just experienced grace."

Tim Keller tells the story of a conversation with an older woman who occasionally attended his church. She was prim and proper—some would even say decent and moral. She turned her nose up at the least bit of impropriety or indiscretion, yet she was not convinced that one had to be saved from anything if one was a good person. In the course of Keller's conversation with her, she said with incredulity, "Now, let me get this straight. You're telling me that if I lead a really good and decent life, and even attend church, but never receive Christ as my Savior, I would be no better off than someone who committed murder? Is *that* what you're saying?"

Keller answered, "Basically, yes."

She retorted, "That's the stupidest religion I've ever heard of!"

To which Keller responded, "Well, maybe you think that it's the stupidest religion you've ever heard of, but for that murderer who is repentant, it's the greatest thing he's ever heard. That former murderer can't believe there's a religion that holds out hope for somebody like him."

While this story is somewhat extreme, it makes an important point. That prim and proper and moral woman who is absolutely sure she is better than most people and who thinks the essence of the gospel is insulting, if not stupid, is herself in the grip of the flesh.[10] She is trying to be decent and upright, but she is trying to do it independently of trusting Christ for her salvation. That is the imminent trap of self-righteousness. Recognizing this great danger, Dietrich Bonhoeffer masterfully describes the attitude of a Christian embraced by grace: "Christians are persons who no longer seek their salvation, their deliverance, their justification in themselves, but in Jesus Christ alone. They know that God's Word in Jesus Christ pronounces them guilty, even when they feel nothing of their own guilt, and that God's Word in Jesus Christ pronounces them free and righteous even when they feel nothing of their own righteousness."[11]

We have not understood the gospel until we understand that God's acceptance of us isn't based on what we have done or ever will do. It is strictly grounded on the nature and character of God to send Jesus into the world, to die for the sins of the world, and to be raised for our salvation.

We are saved by grace. Then, Paul says, grace leads to faith. What is faith? Faith is essentially an awareness of and response to the one who has awakened us.[12] Here is what is critical to understand: the faith that saves us is faith *in* Christ. Christian faith is not general faith in some principles. It is faith that there really was a baby born on Planet Earth who was God in the flesh, who really died on a cross, and who was really raised from the dead. Paul was adamant on this point: "If Christ has not been raised, then our proclamation has been in vain and your faith has been in vain. If Christ has not been raised, your faith is futile and you are still in your sins" (1 Cor. 15:14, 17). If Jesus didn't really die for our sins and didn't really rise from the dead,

---

10. For an in-depth explanation of the meaning of "the flesh," see chapter 4, "Sanctifying Grace."

11. Dietrich Bonhoeffer, *Life Together* (New York: HarperCollins Publishers, 1954), 21–22.

12. I am indebted for this definition to a sermon preached by Tim Keller but cannot recall which sermon it was.

our faith is nothing more than wishful thinking, or moralistic thera-peutic deism.[13] Faith in generalities is pointless.

If Paul were alive today, he might say it like this: *If Jesus is not who he said he is, if he is not the Son of God become human, if he did not really die on the cross for our salvation, if he is not physically raised from the dead, if he has not really ascended into heaven and been seated at the right hand of God the Father, then let's stop playing church.* None of the principles make any sense in and of themselves. Faith in faith? Faith in generalities? No. Because faith in truth and faith in love and faith in justice will not change us or give us new life. It is faith in Jesus. We are not saved by our works, our goodness, or our principles. We are saved because of Christ and Christ alone. Faith in him is what matters because he is our only hope.

Then, faith produces good works. Good works do not save us—not even close. But good works flow out of our faith. It is impossible to say we have received the grace of God and that we have true bib-lical faith if there is nothing different about our lives. The Bible is very practical on this point. We are saved by grace, but if there isn't something actually happening in our concrete character and existing behavior, then it's not real faith. Because, while grace leads to faith, faith leads to good works. "For we are what he has made us, created in Christ Jesus for good works, which God prepared beforehand to be our way of life" (Eph. 2:10).

Christians are God's handiwork. *Poiema* is the Greek word for "what he has made us," or "handiwork." This word is where we get the English word "poem." Christians are uniquely God's poems—God's works of art. Art is beautiful, art is valuable, and art is an expression

---

13. "Moralistic therapeutic deism" is a phrase introduced by Christian Smith and Melinda Lundquist Denton to describe American teenagers at the turn of the twen-ty-first century, and the resultant cultural framework of how postmodern people think about God. Smith and Denton, *Soul Searching: The Religious and Spiritual Lives of Amer-ican Teenagers* (New York: Oxford University Press, 2005).

of the inner being of the artist. What does it mean for Paul to say that Christians are God's artwork? In Christ, we are seen as beautiful, perceived as valuable, and created to be an expression of our Maker, the Divine Artist.

Nevertheless, we are a work of art that has been marred and defaced by sin. Have you ever seen a marred masterpiece—a master artist's magnum opus defaced? In some ways, the original beauty of the masterpiece makes it a far greater tragedy to see it ruined. If a child takes a marker and draws on the kitchen cabinets, it looks bad. But it is far worse if a vandal spray-paints graffiti over Leonardo da Vinci's *Mona Lisa*. The greatness and rarity of that which has been defaced determines the level of tragedy and the level of horror in our response.

Several years ago, I had the opportunity to visit Rome. I was eager to see the *Pietà* in St. Peter's Basilica. Aware that it was carved by Michelangelo from a single block of marble (the only piece known to be personally signed by Michelangelo), I wanted to study it first-hand. I was disappointed to discover it was set back a good distance from the viewing public, behind ropes and protected by a bulletproof panel. Why these precautions? Because in 1972, on Pentecost Sunday, a mentally disturbed geologist claiming to be Jesus attacked the sculpture with a hammer. Onlookers snatched up many of the marble pieces flying off. Some were returned, but some were not, including Mary's nose, which was later reconstructed from a section of marble cut out of her back. The Italians, along with the rest of the art world, were devastated. How could it ever be restored to its original beauty? They searched the world for master artisans who specialized in restoration. After much time, skill, knowledge, labor, and intensity the restoration project was complete.[14] Very few could recognize that it had ever been damaged.

---

14. A *New York Times* article details a group of journalists who were allowed to climb scaffolding and closely inspect the restored sculpture before the viewing public.

That is what God does for everyone he saves by grace. We are his masterpiece, his beloved magnum opus, and he will not let the damage of sin have the last word. To prove our worth, God not only remakes us in the image of Jesus Christ, but he also gives us work to do in his world. We do this work because God has reworked us. When we know this deep in our bones, when we really understand it, we can never again say our good works save us. Moralism can never again be our best response. Our good works are the byproduct of what God has done in us. They reflect God's glory, not our own.

I appreciate the insights Eugene Peterson offers in his paraphrase of Paul's grace equation:

Now God has us where he wants us, with all the time in this world and the next to shower grace and kindness upon us in Christ Jesus. Saving is all his idea, and all his work. All we do is trust him enough to let him do it. It's God's gift from start to finish! We don't play the major role. If we did, we'd probably go around bragging that we'd done the whole thing! No, we neither make nor save ourselves. God does both the making and saving. He creates each of us by Christ Jesus to join him in the work he does, the good work he has gotten ready for us to do, work we had better be doing.

(Eph. 2:7–10, MSG)

God in Christ saves us from condemnation, judgment, and hell.

God in Christ redeems us, and we are fully reconciled.

God in Christ justifies us, making right what was wrong.

"The reconstruction of the damaged veil, eye area, nose, arm and hand looked faultless, except for tiny lines that were visible only in close inspection. There was no perceptible difference in the color of the repaired parts and the surrounding marble surface of the sculpture. 'We worked like dentists,' said Deoclecio Redig de Campos." Paul Hoffman, "Restored Pieta Show; Condition Near Perfect" New York Times, January 5, 1973, https://www.nytimes.com/1973/01/05/archives/restored-pieta-shown-condition-near-perfect-marks-on-marys-cheek.html.

God in Christ remakes us, and we are born again.

God in Christ adopts us into his family.

We are not saved because we put our faith in a doctrine. We are not saved by our right belief. We are saved because something from the outside—or, better, some*one*—has come into us. We are so totally remade that the best way the Gospel writers can think to describe it is to compare it to being born anew. The Hebrew writers described it as the experience of being snatched out of a pit. We were in slavery, and now we are free. We are no longer slaves to fear. We become a child of God. Before we were outside the family of God, and now we are full-blooded members of God's family. We are justified before the Father, which means things are put right.

Let us never forget that salvation comes from the outside, not from within ourselves. We are not saved because we are good; we are saved because God is good. That is what salvation is. God does something for us we couldn't do for ourselves. It is saving grace.

We now turn to what the masterpiece of a renewed life in Christ can fully become by the gift of sanctifying grace.

△□○
THE LIFE

*Through **sanctifying grace**, the Holy Spirit empowers us to live a life fully consecrated to God.*

*Through **sustaining grace**, the Holy Spirit cooperates with us to enable a faithful and disciplined life given in service to God.*

*Through **sufficient grace**, God's power is made perfect in our weakness.*

4
SANCTIFYING GRACE

May the God of peace himself sanctify you entirely; and may your spirit and soul and body be kept sound and blameless at the coming of our Lord Jesus Christ. The one who calls you is faithful, and he will do this.
—1 Thessalonians 5:23–24

According to John Wesley the four most important doctrines found in Scripture are original sin, justification by faith, new birth, and inward and outward holiness.

Justification was a major theme of the Protestant Reformation, which preceded Wesley by nearly two hundred years. The Reformers, including Martin Luther, proclaimed that we are justified with God by faith alone.[1] Wesley strongly affirmed the necessity of justification, but by adding new birth to his list of most important biblical doctrines, he was conveying the essential idea that the cross and resurrection deal decisively with the guilt of our sins and with the core

---

1. Justification is to be made right with God, by the grace of God, by which our sins are forgiven and our guilt removed by the atoning sacrifice of Jesus's death on the cross. See chapter 3, "Saving Grace."

problem that causes us to sin. Thus, for Wesley, new birth is the beginning of the holy life—or, what we call "sanctification."

In the last chapter we discussed the nature of sin and the damaging effects sin has on our world and in our lives. But what is the origin of sin? What is the source of sin in our hearts?

The Bible says sin originates from our inborn nature. "All of us once lived among them in the passions of *our flesh*, following the desires of flesh and senses, and we were *by nature* children of wrath, like everyone else" (Eph. 2:3, emphases added). This verse draws attention to two key phrases that are widely misunderstood and need unpacking for greater understanding.

By Nature

Throughout his New Testament letters, Paul explicitly teaches that human beings are born with a disobedient and sinful nature (Rom. 7:18, 35; Eph. 2:1–3; Col. 3:5). We do not learn to sin. Nobody has to teach us to sin. There is no Sinning 101 class to attend. It comes naturally, and we are good at it. This is not a popular view now, nor has it ever been.

Born in the fourth century, Pelagius was an Irish monk who later became a Roman citizen. He taught that people did not have a sinful nature but that children *learn* to be sinful by the bad examples that are set for them when they are young. Pelagius argued that we are born with a neutral nature and that children become either good or bad due in large part to their models. Therefore, according to Pelagius, sins are deliberate actions of the will, and if we apply our best efforts, we can live very good lives apart from sin.

Pelagius lived during the time of another prominent theologian, Augustine of Hippo, who is considered one of the most influential Christian thinkers in the history of the Western church. The North African bishop wrote extensively about the existence of original sin inherited from our first spiritual parents and its debilitating effects.

Augustine argued strongly against Pelagius's view, calling it contrary to both Scripture and common sense, and he was instrumental in running Pelagius out of the church under the charge of heresy. Although branded by the church as a heretical teaching ever since the fourth century, Pelagianism is alive and well in the church today.

On a trip to New York City, my wife and I attended the Broadway show *Wicked*, which tells the story of Elphaba, the future Wicked Witch of the West (of *The Wizard of Oz* fame), and of her friendship with Glinda, the Good Witch of the North. The story narrates how each woman struggles to find her identity, but eventually Elphaba chooses to be wicked, and Glinda chooses to be good—all because of the circumstances of their lives. Elphaba has bad things happen to her, so she becomes bad; Glinda has things go right for her, so she becomes good. It is only a fictional musical, but countless modern people are prone to think that way about sin.

Jesus, however, does not agree: "But what comes out of the mouth proceeds from the heart, and this is what defiles. For out of the heart come evil intentions, murder, adultery, fornication, theft, false witness, slander" (Matt. 15:18–19). The heart is the source that defiles; sin comes from the heart.

You see a small child, barely old enough to walk. Why do they act the way they do? Why are they selfish? Why do they throw temper tantrums when they don't get their way? A child is not a sinner because of their upbringing. They haven't lived long enough for their examples to affect them to that degree. A child is a sinner because sin comes from the heart—it is inbred. They don't have to be taught to be selfish—they do it naturally. Sin on display is an expression of what is already inside a person. David confessed this: "Indeed, I was born guilty, a sinner when my mother conceived me" (Ps. 51:5). It is the empirical fact of original sin.

What does this look like theologically? Every person is created in the image of God, and God is holy and good. As originally created, humanity reflected the divine nature, but the source of holiness and goodness was not ourselves—it was the eternal, triune God. As explained by William Greathouse and Ray Dunning: "Only God is essentially holy. We are holy only as we are rightly related to God and filled with his sanctifying Spirit." Thus, since the introduction of sin from the fall and its subsequent consequences, our essential nature in the image of God remains intact while the moral image of God is wrecked.[2] Greathouse and Dunning continue, "*Essentially* man is good, a person made for God. *Existentially* man is sinful, a rebel alienated from the life of God and therefore corrupt."[3] Essentially good, existentially rebellious. This is original sin.

We have a nature we are born with. It is not a "thing" in us needing to be removed, like a bad gallbladder. It is our disposition toward pride and self-centeredness. It is our inborn tendency toward violence, ego, self-sufficiency, and self-preservation. It is narcissism of the highest order and in its most obvious form—which means sin in our hearts is more than a few indiscretions we commit in our worst moments; it is disregard of the first commandment (Exod. 20:3) and

---

2. *Imago Dei* is the Latin translation of "image of God." While the moral image of God in humanity is damaged as a consequence of the fall, the essential nature of God maintains the value of every person made in the image of God. Diane LeClerc notes that Nazarene theologian Mildred Bangs Wynkoop, faithful to the teaching of John Wesley, "defines the image of God in humanity as the capacity to love, in the context of a relationship with God, others, self, and the earth." LeClerc, *Discovering Christian Holiness: The Heart of Wesleyan-Holiness Theology* (Kansas City, MO: Beacon Hill Press of Kansas City, 2010), 312. Also, see the final section of this chapter, "Defining Entire Sanctification."

3. Greathouse and Dunning, *An Introduction to Wesleyan Theology* (Kansas City, MO: Beacon Hill Press of Kansas City, 1982), 52. They go on to detail the *historical* meaning of original sin (Rom. 5:12–21) and the *existential* meaning of original sin (Rom. 7:14–25), 53–54. The Wesleyan perspective of original sin is different from the Calvinist doctrine of total depravity.

The human body is clearly not a bad thing. After all, God created the human body and then took on a human body in Jesus. When Paul wants to refer to the physical body he usually chooses the Greek word *soma*, not *sarx*, which he does thirteen times in Romans alone. The word *soma* can mean either the human physical body or the whole of a person, as in Romans 12:1: "present your bodies as a living sacrifice, holy and acceptable to God," which is a clear call to the sanctification of our whole person, including our physical bodies.

So what is the flesh, and why is sanctifying grace needed? The flesh is the bent of the whole person (body, mind, and spirit) to be our own god, rather than coming under the lordship of Jesus. It is the sinful aspect of our self that wants to live our lives independent of God—to be our own king and savior, rather than depending on Jesus. Prior to saving grace, we are completely controlled by the flesh instead of the Spirit. We have a sinful nature—a heart disposition that believes we can save ourselves, and that is totally consumed and dominated by the mind of the flesh. However, at the moment of our justification (pardon for sin) and regeneration (new birth), we are given the gift of the Holy Spirit.[10] Wesleyan-Holiness people also refer to this as "initial sanctification" because we cannot be given that which is holy—the Spirit of Jesus—and not begin the journey of the holy life ourselves.[11]

This is where the war for sovereignty begins. Who will be king of my life? Before we were Christians there was no war—not even an occasional skirmish. The flesh that was committed to our self-sover-

10. While "regeneration" is not a biblical word *per se*, theologians have created the word to describe the new life that is given by grace to a person as a result of their new birth in Christ. In a very real sense, one is raised to a new life, a spiritual resurrection occurs, and actual changes ensue in tangible and intangible ways.

11. "Wesley never actually used this term [initial sanctification], but it signifies his belief that the moment of salvation begins the process of being made righteous." Leerc, *Discovering Christian Holiness*, 318.

a failure to worship God alone. N. T. Wright reminds us just how deeply immersed we really are:

> The diagnosis of the human plight is not then simply that humans have broken God's moral law, offending and insulting the Creator, whose image they bear—though that is true as well. This lawbreaking is a symptom of a much more serious disease. Morality is important, but it isn't the whole story. Called to responsibility and authority within and over creation, humans have turned their vocation upside down, giving worship and allegiance to forces and powers within creation itself. The name for this is idolatry. The result is slavery and finally death.[4]

We have more than a bad record. We have a fallen nature. God's grace is needed to provide deliverance from and healing of the *condition* of sin and the *acts* of sin—original and actual. For this we need both justification and sanctification. We need to be re-formed and given a radical renovation of our hearts. That is why Wesley emphasized inward and outward holiness. We must be forgiven of our sins, made alive in Christ, and have our hearts purified by faith. The result is a recovery of the full image of God that was lost.

Works of the Flesh

As noted previously, the writings of the New Testament—particularly those attributed to the apostle Paul—often refer to an aspect of the catastrophic fallout of original sin as "works of the flesh." The word "flesh" derives from a single Greek word, *sarx*.[5] Not to be con-

4. N. T. Wright, *The Day the Revolution Began: Reconsidering the Meaning of Jesus's Crucifixion* (New York: HarperCollins Publishers, 2016), 76–77.

5. A two-nature theory of the Christian life was introduced through a widely popular dispensational viewpoint from the late nineteenth and early twentieth centuries that had a far-reaching influence among many evangelicals, including a number of noteworthy evangelical preachers and teachers. This influence led the committee of the earliest (1973) translation of the New International Version to translate "flesh" (*sarx*) as "sinful nature." Dunning points out that Greathouse subsequently suggested that it

fused with the body, the flesh is used in a spiritual sense to refer to the self-centered bent that seeks to be gratified, the inordinate self-love of the "I" that lives for oneself rather than fully surrendering to the will and purposes of God.[6] Martin Luther—and Augustine before him—graphically described this as the state of "being curved in on oneself" (incurvatus in se). Think deeply about the mental picture Luther paints of turning in toward oneself: "Our nature, by the corruption of the first sin, [being] so deeply curved in on itself that it not only bends the best gifts of God towards itself and enjoys them (as is plain in the works-righteous and hypocrites), or rather even uses God himself in order to attain these gifts, but it also fails to realize that it so wickedly, curvedly, and viciously seeks all things, even God, for its own sake."[7]

When Paul says, "I can will what is right, but I cannot do it" (Rom. 7:18b), he is referring to the powerlessness in his flesh to love and obey God with his whole heart. He is, and we are, enslaved to the "I" that wants what we want. Paul expands further in his letter to the Galatians that the flesh wars against the Spirit: "For what the flesh desires is opposed to the Spirit, and what the Spirit desires is opposed to the flesh; for these are opposed to each other, to prevent you from doing what you want" (Gal. 5:17). He then follows by illustrating vivid examples of the works of the flesh and the actions and attitudes that follow the flesh, as contrasted to the fruit of the Spirit (vv. 19–23). Then, as if to drive it home, Paul delivers the knockout

punch: "To set the mind on the flesh is death, but to set the mind on the Spirit is life and peace" (Rom. 8:6). My paraphrase: Either we kill the misdeeds of the flesh, or they are going to kill us. This is the uncensored gravity of the flesh.

The biblical idea of the flesh has been generally misunderstood over the years. Regrettably, some think that flesh and Spirit correspond to body and soul and that "flesh" refers to the skin on our bodies.[8] As a result, some have been led to assume that if the flesh is the source of evil and sin, then our physical bodies must be intrinsically bad. Therefore, as the thinking goes, we should downplay the physical aspects of our lives, beat our bodies into submission, and not allow any physical pleasure or satisfaction.[9] While this may seem extreme, it plays out to some degree whenever a hierarchy of sin is created, such as sins of the body and sins of the spirit, and when we push the idea that one is surely worse than the other (e.g., sexual immorality must be worse than gossip or bitterness; drunkenness must be worse than pride than racism). Consequently, if someone commits a sin of the body—a considered a "mortal" sin—it is nearly unforgiveable, but sins of spirit are brushed off with the justification that "nobody's perfect." separate and classify sin in this manner is a clear misunderstandi scriptural holiness, not to mention the fact that Paul classifies together in one category (e.g., see Gal. 5:16–21: idolatry and g are both identified as "works of the flesh").

was "virtually impossible to use [that version of the translation] as the basis for a faithful interpretation of the original Greek." The 2011 translation committee for the NIV revised its translation to "flesh." Dunning, Pursuing the Divine Image: An Exegetically Based Theology of Holiness (Marrickville, New South Wales: Southwood Press, 2016), Kindle Location 786.

6. Greathouse and Dunning define the flesh as "'I' living for myself." Greathouse and Dunning, An Introduction to Wesleyan Theology, 53.

7. Martin Luther, Lectures on Romans, WA 56:304.

8. The "flesh" and the "body" are two separate words in the New Te and soma.

9. Much of the heresy of Gnosticism is based on a misconception of t sponding to the body. The Platonic idea of an abstract supreme soul ca today to look on the body with contempt and to emphasize the mortal eternal soul. However, this error is in conflict with the biblical doctri urrection. To combat this prevalent misunderstanding, the earliest underscored the importance of bodily resurrection (e.g., "We believe i of the body, and the life everlasting," Apostles' Creed).

eignty and selfish desires dominated us. When the Spirit comes into our life we are given new desires, motivations, and the mind of Christ (Rom. 12:2; 1 Cor. 2:16; Phil. 2:5). These two forces, flesh and Spirit, are in opposition and now fight for supremacy. Holiness is initiated but must now increase and mature.

When Paul wrote to the church in Corinth, he "could not speak to them as spiritual people" (1 Cor. 3:1). Does this mean that they were not Christians? No, they were born-again Christians. In fact, he begins the letter by calling them "those who are sanctified in Christ Jesus," and "called to be saints" (1:2). Regeneration, justification, and redemption had taken place. Their journey of grace had commenced. Their problem was that the battle for their flesh was ongoing. Their envy, rivalry, pride, and divisiveness were still on full display. They were Christians—but still "people of the flesh" (3:1)—which Paul equated with immature faith. They were Christians but still "infants in Christ" (3:1). They had some growing up to do. This is another way to say there was still a level of resistance in them that had not yet fully surrendered their wills and minds to God.[12]

Again, John Wesley offers a keen insight into the context of Paul's statements. Asking if the Corinthians had lost their faith, Wesley insisted, "Nay, he [Paul] manifestly declares they had not; for then they would not have been 'babes in Christ.' And he speaks of being 'carnal' and 'babes in Christ' as one and the same thing; plainly showing that every believer is (in a degree) 'carnal' while he is only a 'babe in Christ.'"[13] Carnal, for Wesley, is the equivalent of being "in the

---

12. "The Greek term translated 'mind' is one of the most significant anthropological terms used by Paul. It refers to the reasoning aspect of a person when the powers of judgment are being exercised." Dunning, *Pursuing the Divine Image*, Kindle Location 814. The God-given capacity of each person to think and use intellect to understand is one aspect of the so-called Wesleyan Quadrilateral known as "reason."

13. John Wesley, Sermon 13: "On Sin in Believers," in *The Complete Works of John Wesley: Vol. 1, Sermons 1–53* (Fort Collins, CO: Delmarva Publications, 2014), 3.2.

flesh," and represents an immature faith that must grow into Christ-likeness and the self-giving way of the cross.[14] This is true for every believer. The question is not salvation—it is lordship. The sanctified must grow more and more into the likeness of Jesus. It is not some *thing* that must die in them—*they* must die, in some real yet figurative sense, to what ruled their lives before.[15] Religious credentials will not suffice; moral standards will not be enough. One must die to one's confidence in the flesh.

In a stunning moment of vulnerable candor, Paul confessed, "If anyone else has reason to be confident in the flesh, I have more: cir-cumcised on the eighth day, a member of the people of Israel, of the tribe of Benjamin, a Hebrew born of Hebrews; as to the law, a Phar-isee; as to zeal, a persecutor of the church; as to righteousness under the law, blameless" (Phil. 3:4b–6). He had all the religious credentials to be considered righteous, but his confidence would have been in the flesh. Paul continues, "Yet whatever gains I had, these I have to come to regard as loss because of Christ" (v. 7). He was keeping the rules and obeying the law, but he was living according to the flesh as long as he believed and depended on his own righteousness to save him or make him holy. They were good things that had been elevated to a central place in his life—thus, he had to die to them so that he might know Christ. And, in knowing Christ more completely and increasingly, Paul traded his hard-earned moral efforts for Christ's

---

14. Dunning makes the point that "carnality is a misleading word, being used as a noun whereas the scripture always uses carnal [fleshly] in an adjectival way." Dunning, *Pursuing the Divine Image*, Kindle Location 2076. This also rejects the idea that "the flesh" is a kind of alien thing, like a "cancerous tumor living metaphorically within us" that must be surgically removed. Ibid., Kindle Location 801. Proponents of the con-cept of something needing to be removed, including some nineteenth-century Holiness preachers, refer to this as eradication.

15. William H. Greathouse with George Lyons, *New Beacon Bible Commentary, Romans 1–8: A Commentary in the Wesleyan Tradition* (Kansas City, MO: Beacon Hill Press of Kansas City, 2008), 182.

saving and sanctifying righteousness: "in order that I may gain Christ and be found in him, not having a righteousness of my own that comes from the law, but one that comes through faith in Christ, the righteousness from God based on faith" (vv. 8b–9).

Many people are moral, even religious, but condescension, rigidity, prejudice, harshness, and coldness of spirit are telltale signs that the flesh has taken religion and used it as a strategy to avoid depending on Jesus Christ for one's holiness. As a greedy businessman whose exploitation of those trapped in poverty in order to make a profit is under the bondage of the flesh, so is the Pharisee. In God's eyes, they are the same. They are both people who have undertaken strategies to forge their own way in life apart from God.

Here is the difficult truth: even Christians can continue to live according to the flesh. Before saving grace, the flesh does not war with the Spirit because we are dead in our sins. Yet even when the Spirit of God comes alive in us we can still live in a fleshly way. We can still take good things and make them ultimate things. We can still live in our own strength and power, instead of depending on God's. That is why we need sanctifying grace. We need God's grace to crucify the flesh that wants to depend on ourselves—to put to death the fleshly part of us that wants to manage our own lives in order that the Spirit of Jesus can take complete control.[16]

Acclaimed Scottish teacher and devotional writer Oswald Chambers gets to the heart of dying to self so that Christ might be known more and more:

I must take my emotional opinions and intellectual beliefs and be willing to turn them into a moral verdict against the nature

---

16. Oswald Chambers refers to the notion of dying to self as identification with the death of Jesus and a willing "co-crucifixion." In the same way, the Christian can be united with Jesus in his resurrection and share a "co-resurrection" to new life. The resurrection life of Jesus is experienced now in the life of holiness. Chambers, My Utmost for His Highest (Uhrichsville, OH: Barbour and Company, 1935), 73.

of sin; that is, against any claim I have to my right to myself. . . . Once I reach this moral decision and act on it, all that Christ accomplished *for* me on the cross is accomplished *in* me. My unrestrained commitment of myself to God gives the Holy Spirit the opportunity to grant me the holiness of Jesus Christ. . . . My individuality remains, but my primary motivation for living and the nature that rules me are radically changed.[17]

The flesh does not have to rule our lives. Freedom is offered for a holy life. Sanctifying grace is the means and the remedy. So how does sanctifying grace actually work in the journey of grace? To that end, we give the remainder of the chapter.

Becoming Like Jesus

I want to tell a story about someone I am going to call George (not his real name). George was a member of my church and a very unhappy person. He was always upset about something. He did not like the music or my preaching. He said I didn't preach holiness in the way he heard it as a kid. Moreover, he didn't particularly like people—especially new people. George wrote me seven-page letters containing some of the ugliest comments you could imagine, not only attacking every move I made in my pastorate but also assuming to know my motives.

For a while his complaints were that the church was inward-focused and not reaching out. Then, when the church began to fill with new people, he didn't like that either because now, he said, we didn't care anymore for the folks who had been there for years and who had paid the price for the church to become stable. He said we were only growing because we were stealing sheep from other churches (which was not true). The bottom line was that George didn't want things to change.

---

17. Chambers, *My Utmost for His Highest*, 58.

George consumed so much of my emotional energy as a pastor. He repeatedly threatened to leave the church. I think deep down inside he knew what we all knew—that no other church would tolerate him. Finally, one day I called him and said, "George, you know I love you, but no more letters or emails. I cannot hear your heart in an email, and you cannot hear mine. From now on, if you have a concern or complaint, you're going to have to say it face to face."

It seemed as if things got better—at least for a while. He never did send me another letter, but he continued to spread negativity in the church. It got to the point that George was more like a mosquito than an attack dog—more annoying than dangerous.

The saddest part for me was that George was not being transformed. He was a cranky person and had been for as long as anyone could remember. It was not just at church. He wasn't a good husband to his wife, his children didn't want to be around him, and he had no joy in his life. Most surprising, he had been attending church his entire sixty-plus years. Perhaps worst of all, nobody was surprised that he wasn't changing, and nobody was even particularly bothered by it. They had accepted it. "Oh, that's just the way George is," they would say. No one expected him to become more like Jesus.

In thinking about George, I have come to believe that the wrong question to ask about the health of a church is, "How many people are attending?" The better question, or at least moving in the right direction, is to ask, "What are these people like?"[18] When someone becomes a Christian, the goal is not only to learn how to follow Christ but actually to live a Christlike life. This is the goal of all discipleship on the journey of grace.

---

18. Bill Hull, *The Disciple-Making Pastor* (Old Tappan, NJ: Revell, 1988), 13.

The Goal of Discipleship

When Paul set forth the gifts of ministry, he said there would be apostles, prophets, evangelists, pastors, and teachers but that their unified purpose would be "to equip the saints for the work of ministry, for building up the body of Christ" (Eph. 4:12). There is a lot to unpack in those words relative to discipleship, but let's start with the concept of "body."

The body is an intriguing analogy because whenever spiritual growth is mentioned there is the assumption that something is alive. All living things grow. Dead things stay static or decay. Only living things grow. Inanimate things do not grow. A piece of furniture doesn't grow. A rock doesn't grow. Only organisms grow.

An organism can be (1) a living thing such as a plant, animal, or person, or (2) a functioning system of interdependent parts that comprise a living creature or thing. Plants are organisms. Plants cannot grow without sunlight, water, and nutrients. They need an ecosystem to sustain their growth, or they die. Our human bodies are also organisms. The human anatomy is a system of functioning interdependent parts—an operational system designed to work together: "the body is one and has many members" (1 Cor. 12:12a). When one of our *parts* is not working correctly, regardless of how insignificant it may seem, it can throw the entire system off and cause us to become unhealthy.

When Paul says that we are the body of Christ, he is making the point that the church is also an organism, composed of dynamic, living people who are interdependent parts working together and depending on each other for vitality and health by the power of the Holy Spirit: "Indeed, the body does not consist of one member but of many" (1 Cor. 12:14). When the parts are not working together in a holistic way, it becomes sick and weak. Conversely, when the parts are connected and growing together in nourishing ways, vitality and health are the result, a shape begins to form, and an end goal (*telos*) is achieved. We build up the body, "until all of us come to the unity of the faith and of the knowledge of the Son of God, to *maturity*, to the measure of the *full stature of Christ*" (Eph. 4:13, emphases added). The goal of Christian maturity is the full stature of Christ—Christlikeness. There is no other aim. So it is for the church. When our individual members come together, it is to look like the body of Christ. And, just in case we missed it the first time, Paul reiterates that "we must grow up in every way into him who is the head, into Christ, from whom the whole body" grows into what it is intended to be (v. 15b–16a).

The goal of all spiritual growth, individually and communally, personally and corporately, is to become more and more like Jesus. The act or process of becoming like Jesus is sanctification, and is made possible by sanctifying grace.

Holiness Is Not Optional

In the Greek language, sanctification is related to the word "holy" (*hagios*). Wesleyan-Holiness theology maintains that the good news of the gospel is not only that we will one day be with God when we die but also that the offer of abundant life in God's kingdom is for now, right where we are. God's plan is that his image in us that was marred by the fall should be restored to all of its beauty and glory, that we would become his masterpiece, reflecting Christlikeness in what we think, say, and do. That is called sanctification, and that is what we are becoming. It is not optional for a growing Christian.

When people buy a car they are informed by the salesperson that there is *standard* equipment and *optional* accessories. They know they are going to get a steering wheel and seatbelts and rearview mirrors because that is *standard* equipment—every car has them. However, if they want automatic windows, alloy wheels, and a sunroof, they have to ask because those are *optional* accessories, meaning not every car has them. Sanctification is not an optional accessory for a disciple of Jesus. It is standard equipment for every model. Becoming like Jesus is expected because growth is not an option. We are always growing toward something—always in the process of being spiritually formed.

Again, Paul affirms this in Romans 12 when he says, "Do not be conformed to this world, but be transformed by the renewing of your minds, so that you may discern what is the will of God—what is good and acceptable and perfect" (v. 2). Conformed or *transformed*— those are our only two alternatives. If we are not being transformed (changed from the inside out) by the renewing power of God, then we are being conformed (shaped and molded) by forces opposed to God that are loose in the world. The question is not *if* you are going to be spiritually formed; the question is what *will* form you? If God is not forming us, there is a spiritual enemy—an adversary, the evil one—who is perfectly happy to configure our lives.

Simply put, the world apart from God *de*forms and *mal*forms people. God *re*forms and *trans*forms. That is why sanctification—becoming like Jesus—is so important. Few words better summarize God's will for human life than these from Scripture: "For this is the will of God, your sanctification" (1 Thess. 4:3a); and "Pursue peace with everyone, and the holiness without which no one will see the Lord" (Heb. 12:14). The command to pursue peace and holiness implies action over passivity. The spiritual growth of a person is called sanctification, or holiness. Initial sanctification and entire sanctification are not the same, but the goal of all sanctification is to become like Jesus. This is God's will for every Christian's life because, if we do not "grow up in every way into him who is the head, into Christ," we are being formed by something other than holy love (Eph. 4:15).

An Equation for Spiritual Growth

Discipleship is not an option. Most Christians would not argue that point. The real question is, how does this growth take place? In his book *Rethinking the Church*, James Emery White explains what many people believe about the discipleship process. The formula he offers is given in the form of a math equation:

Salvation + Time + Individual Application = Life Change

The formula develops based on four assumptions: (1) life change happens at salvation; (2) it continues to occur naturally over time; (3) it is achieved largely by an act of the will; and (4) it is best accomplished alone.[19] Let's look carefully at the proposed hypothesis.

First, "salvation." Salvation is such a radical transformation of our being ("born again") that there is an immediate change of heart that issues in a miraculous conversion of desires, habits, attitudes, and character. Christians are born, *not* made. Since salvation changes the status of our relationship with God, alters our eternal destiny, and introduces the power and work of the Holy Spirit in our lives, immediate and substantive growth is expected. That is the assumption of salvation.

Second, "time." While the transformation process takes place at conversion, it is obvious that a person is not fully grown when they become a Christian. There are still remaining pockets of resistance and selfishness that need to be dealt with, White says, but those are things cared for in the passage of time.[20] Therefore, the formula follows that a five-year Christian will have five years of spiritual maturity and a ten-year Christian will have ten years of maturity, and so on. Faith cannot help but grow with time, so all we have to do is read the Bible and attend church as much as possible, and the fruit of the Spirit will multiply, and we will become more like Jesus. That is the assumption of time.

---

19. James Emery White, *Rethinking the Church: A Challenge to Creative Redesign in an Age of Transition* (Grand Rapids: Baker Books, 1997), 55.

20. White, *Rethinking the Church*, 56.

Third, "individual application." This has to do with a person's willpower. The idea is that whatever does not happen naturally over time will be supplemented by determination and human effort. All a person must do is decide to live and act in a certain way (and throw in a little perseverance)—because the Christian life is sustained by acts of the will. Enough time plus our willpower will produce the fruit of the Spirit. That is the assumption of individual application.

Finally, "best accomplished alone." The final assumption of the equation of discipleship is independence, or that a personal relationship with Jesus Christ is tantamount to a private one.[21]

Thus the equation goes, but we rarely bother to ask if those assumptions are valid. Is that how discipleship happens? Do we *automatically* begin to grow in our spiritual life after salvation? When someone becomes a Christian is there an immediate, in-depth change of habits, attitudes, and character transformation? Do Christians grow by time alone and willpower alone? Because our relationship with God is personal, are disciples of Jesus better off working solo? If these assumptions are correct, there should be ample evidence of it in the church. If they are true, White points out, then simply working the equation should consistently offer the same results: individual Christians and the body of Christ becoming more and more like Jesus in our thinking, speaking, and acting.[22] However, there are important reasons why the formula is not altogether complete.

For starters, disciples of Jesus are both born *and* made. Saving grace changes our relational status with God, our eternal destiny, and introduces the power and work of the Holy Spirit into our lives. But, as we see from New Testament teachings, new Christians are

---

21. The idea of a personal relationship with Christ being synonymous with a private relationship with Jesus is far more prevalent in Western society than other parts of the world. Individualism is considered a cultural virtue in the USA.

22. White, *Rethinking the Church*, 57.

not yet mature in character. *Being* a Christian does not automatically translate into *becoming* like Christ. Development is needed. Virtue is grown over time through specific practices.[23] In light of these actualities, let's consider a more biblical framework of how spiritual growth takes place through sanctifying grace.

1. Spiritual growth may begin at salvation, but we continue to grow in grace throughout our lives. There is a difference between sanctification and entire sanctification. The debate always seems to be whether sanctification is instantaneous or gradual. Is there a crisis moment, or is it a process? The answer is both.[24] Sanctifying grace begins the moment we experience saving grace. Theologians refer to it as "initial sanctification," which is followed by spiritual growth in grace, until—in a moment of full consecration and complete surrender on our part—God purifies and cleanses the heart. This is an experience referred to as entire sanctification, or "Christian perfection."[25] However, even following that moment of full consecration to

---

23. N. T. Wright defines the Christian concept of virtue as the transformation of character. Wright, *After You Believe: Why Christian Character Matters* (New York: HarperCollins Publishers, 2010). Much more time will be given to an understanding of virtue in chapter 5, "Sustaining Grace."

24. The subject of instantaneous or progressive, crisis or process, in the experience of entire sanctification has historically been a topic of great debate in Wesleyan-Holiness circles. John Wesley himself consistently emphasized the need for both, and early Nazarene leaders were generally careful to suggest a balance. General Superintendent R. T. Williams stated the following to the 1928 General Assembly of the Church of the Nazarene: "The church must place emphasis both upon the crisis and the process in religion. . . . For many years the holiness people felt that the work to which they were called ended at the altar, when the crowds who came forward received the blessing of regeneration and sanctification, but it became evident that our work has only begun at this point. . . . The Church of the Nazarene is combining these two great principles, namely the crisis and the process. Leading [people] to God and the edification of the body of Christ in initial salvation and the development of Christian character." *General Assembly Journal*, 1928, referenced in Dunning, *Pursuing the Divine Image*, Kindle Location 2176, footnote 26.

25. Christian perfection is a biblical and often-used phrase throughout Christian history. Early church fathers and mothers equated perfection with the idea of *theosis*, or deification: partaking of the divine nature. However, the modern concept of perfection

God, we continue to grow in grace and never stop growing as long as we live.

The Articles of Faith for the Church of the Nazarene state: "We believe there is a marked distinction between a pure heart and a mature character. The former is obtained in an instant, the result of entire sanctification; the latter is the result of growth in grace." When we respond in faith to prevenient grace, we receive saving grace. There is a radical reorientation of our priorities, a reconstituting of our desires, and the power and work of the Holy Spirit are set loose in our lives. Rather than instant liberation from every harmful habit, character flaw, or bad disposition we have ever possessed, God continues to work in us to shape us into who he wants us to be. The goal of all Christian discipleship is becoming more and more like Jesus. That's why Paul reasons, just as we don't expect babies to remain babies, just as we want them to grow and mature into fully functioning adults, we should also expect as Christians not to stay spiritual babies either. Spiritual growth begins at salvation, but we continue to grow in grace through our whole lives. We should look, act, and think more like Christ next year than we do today, so we progress by sanctifying grace.

2. Spiritual growth involves more than just time. Either most of my friends do not know, or they have forgotten, that I can play the piano. I have been playing the piano for more than forty years. When I was ten, I practiced almost every day (with a lot of supervision from

---

is understood differently. It has never accurately been taught as a "sinless perfection," or, as Thomas Noble writes, "the idea that within this life, Christians could reach that final, absolute state of perfection where they were sinless and perfectly holy." T. A. Noble, *Holy Trinity, Holy People: The Historic Doctrine of Christian Perfecting* (Eugene, OR: Cascade Books, 2013), 22. To avoid the confusion of modern interpretation, and to highlight the dynamic aspects of growth in grace, Noble contends, "Given that dynamic concept of the perfection of movement, rather than final arrival, it may be preferable to express this meaning of the Greek word not by using the word 'perfection,' but by translating it as 'perfecting.'" Ibid., 24.

my mother, who prioritized piano practice over football). Now I play with much less frequency—about once a year. If someone were to ask me how long I have played, it would be truthful for me to say four decades, but the rest of the story is that I haven't spent all of those four decades being intentional about practicing. There are children at church who have only played the piano for a few years who can play better than I can, even though I have technically been playing much longer.

It is no different with our spiritual lives. Simply being exposed to information doesn't mean that people absorb it, understand it, embrace it, and live it. While it is true that spiritual growth takes time, it is not true that sanctifying grace is inherently a product of time, or even a byproduct of exposure to Christian culture.[26] Churches are full of people who have spent years being Christians—yet their lives reflect very little of the Spirit of Jesus. They are critical, cranky, cynical, negative, and selfish. Many of them are just like George from one of my former congregations: they are not becoming more and more like Jesus every year. The reason is very simple.

3. Spiritual growth is not so much a question of time, as it is cooperation with God and intentional training. The writer to the Hebrews says, "For though by this time you ought to be teachers, you need someone to teach you again the basic elements of the oracles of God. You need milk, not solid food; for everyone who lives on milk, being still an infant, is unskilled in the word of righteousness. But solid food is for the mature, for those whose faculties have been *trained by practice* to distinguish good from evil. Therefore let us go on toward perfection, leaving behind the basic teaching about Christ" (Heb. 5:12–6:1a, emphasis added).[27] Based on the phrase "by

---

26. White, *Rethinking the Church*, 59.

27. Wesley was fond of describing sanctification as Christian perfection, even titling his most famous doctrinal catechism *A Plain Account of Christian Perfection*. In argu-

this time," we can assume this part of Scripture was written to believers who had been Christians for some time already. Instead of becoming *teachers* of the journey of grace through their words and their example, they were still eating baby food. The path to eating a grown-up diet and becoming a mature Christian is through *training* themselves in righteousness—training that would help them recognize the difference between right and wrong and distinguish between good and better. This is going on toward Christian perfection, or a maturity in Christ that allows repentant believers to turn aside from aspects of the flesh that yet remain in the heart.[28]

The phrase "trained by practice" in the Hebrews scripture is intriguing. It implies intentional effort, and it implies that Christians participate in our own spiritual growth in Christ. Other examples abound: "Equip yourself! Build up your faith! Run the race! Guard your heart!" These are all biblical mandates to work out in the world what God is working in us. This training is accomplished by specific practices—or means of grace—that John Wesley called works of pi-

---

ing that the experience of perfect love, or "God perfecting in love," can be realized in this life, he points out: "(1) there is such a thing as perfection; for it is again and again mentioned in Scripture. (2) It is not so early as justification; for justified persons are to 'go on to perfection.' (Heb. 6:1) (3) It is not so late as death; for St. Paul speaks of living men that were perfect. (Phil. 3:15)." Wesley, *A Plain Account of Christian Perfection, Annotated*, eds. Randy L. Maddox and Paul W. Chilcote (Kansas City, MO: Beacon Hill Press of Kansas City, 2015).

28. John Wesley, in a sermon titled "The Repentance of Believers," stressed the continuing necessity of repentance for Christians who would pursue the holy life. In a paper delivered at a holiness conference, one of my theology professors from seminary, Dr. Rob L. Staples, said, "Entire sanctification can be understood as a total commitment to our destiny of *theosis* [renewal in the image of God] with a continual repentance for, and resultant cleansing from, anything that impedes or dilutes such commitment, or what Wesley called 'the repentance of believers' which he said is 'requisite in every subsequent stage of our Christian course.'" Staples, "Things Shakable and Things Unshakable in Holiness Theology," Revisioning Holiness Conference, Northwest Nazarene University, February 9, 2007.

ety and works of mercy.[29] Works of piety include the instituted means of grace such as prayer, reading the Bible, fasting, receiving the Lord's Supper, baptism, and spending time with other Christians. Works of mercy are also a means of grace while in service to others, such as "feeding the hungry, clothing the naked, entertaining the stranger, visiting those who are in prison or the sick, and instructing the uninformed."[30] We *practice* the means of grace even as we receive them as gifts; our participation is required.[31]

Nevertheless, we must be careful not to confuse participation with control. We do not control our spiritual growth—or even cause it. There are some things within our control. We can make a phone call, wash our clothes, or run an errand. There are also things about which we can do nothing. We cannot change the weather. We cannot change our genes. There are things we can control and those we cannot—both exist.

However, there is also a third category: the things we do not control but can cooperate with. Think about sleep. If you have ever had children, you may be familiar with having to tell them to go to sleep. Sometimes they will respond by saying, "I can't!" And they are partially right. They cannot *make* themselves go to sleep in the same way you can make a phone call. As parents, we assure our kids they can do some things to open themselves up to sleep. They can prepare for sleep. They can lie down in bed, turn out the lights, close their eyes, listen to soft music, and sleep will come! They cannot control

---

29. "By 'means of grace' I understand outward signs, words, or actions, ordained of God, and appointed for this end, to be the ordinary channels whereby he might convey to men, preventing, justifying, or sanctifying grace." Wesley, "Sermon 16: The Means of Grace," II.1, http://wesley.nnu.edu/john-wesley/the-sermons-of-john-wesley-1872-edition/sermon-16-the-means-of-grace/. Means of grace are also called spiritual disciplines.

30. Joel B. Green and William H. Willimon, eds., *Wesley Study Bible New Revised Standard Version* (Nashville: Abingdon Press, 2009), 1488, footnote "Going on to Perfection."

31. For more on the means of grace, see chapter 5, "Sustaining Grace."

it, but they are not helpless. They can open themselves up to sleep and let it quietly sneak up on them. The same is true of spiritual growth. We cannot sanctify ourselves or make ourselves like Jesus. The Holy One makes us holy. God is our sanctifier. But, as in our salvation, cooperation is necessary. We do not save ourselves, but we must say yes to saving grace.

Eminent discipleship teacher Dallas Willard famously said, "Grace is not opposed to effort; it is opposed to earning."[32] Grace is for more than regeneration, justification, and forgiveness. Grace is needed for the entire journey of discipleship. Even so, perhaps the great danger of our time is not to think we are doing too much in our discipleship journey but to assume we have to do nothing. Passivity can be as dangerous as legalism. When Paul says to take off the old self and put on the new, he surely means we must do it with God's help. Paul is uncompromising on this: "Train yourself in godliness" (1 Tim. 4:7), and again, "Do you not know that in a race the runners all compete, but only one receives the prize? Run in such a way that you may win it" (1 Cor. 9:24).

Grace means God has done everything we could not do for ourselves, but it does not mean we now become consumers who contribute nothing to the relationship. This mistaken idea accounts for the hands-off discipleship approach of many Christians and, as a result, the lack of spiritual growth and maturity. Thus, Dallas Willard also said, "We know, as Jesus says, 'Without me you can do nothing' (John 15:5). . . . But we had better believe that the back side of that verse reads, 'If you do nothing it will be without me.' And this is the part we have the hardest time hearing."[33] We cooperate with the active grace of God by reordering our lives around those activities, disciplines, and practices

---

32. Dallas Willard, *The Great Omission: Reclaiming Jesus's Essential Teachings on Discipleship* (New York: HarperCollins, 2006), 61.

33. Willard, "Spiritual Formation: What It Is, and How It Is Done," n.d., http://www.dwillard.org/articles/individual/spiritual-formation-what-it-is-and-how-it-is-done.

that were modeled by Jesus Christ. And we participate in them not to earn our sanctification but in order to accomplish through training what we cannot do by merely "trying harder."

4. Spiritual growth is a communal effort. Western readers tend to be surprised by the communal emphasis of Paul's description of the journey of grace, though many non-Western cultures already know that we cannot travel the road alone. Reading again from his crowning theological treatise relative to the church: "He [Christ] makes the whole body fit together perfectly. As each part does its own special work, *it helps the other parts grow*, so that the whole body is healthy and growing and full of love" (Eph. 4:16, NLT, emphasis added). As unexpected as these verses might be to cultures accustomed to bowing at the altar of individualism, including individualistic spirituality, Paul is unapologetic that our discipleship was never intended to be a solo act. Each "part" (individual) of the body is important and has a unique work to do, but the all the individual work has a combined stated purpose: to help the other parts grow.

It is holy synergy. "Synergy" comes from the Greek word *synergos*, which means "working together." It has been said that the work of a whole is greater than the individual sum of its parts, or that the combination of individual parts produces a greater impact than one could do alone. Synergy is found in nature, business, sports, and family relationships. It is the power of interdependence, reciprocity, and mutuality.[34]

A popular example of mutuality is the relationship between zebras and very small birds called oxpeckers. The oxpeckers eat the ticks on the backs of zebras, acting as a kind of pest control; the ox-

---

34. For more on a biblical understanding of interdependence, see Paul's New Testament teaching on the human body as a metaphor for the church (1 Corinthians 12, Ephesians 4). For more on mutuality, see his teaching on Christian marriage (Ephesians 5).

peckers also make a hissing sound when they are frightened, serving as an alarm system for the zebras when predators are nearby. The zebras supply plenty of food for the birds; the birds supply the zebras with good hygiene and healthcare. These two animals are completely different in so many ways, but they each need the other to thrive.

Synergy is also the measure of a healthy body that is growing and full of perfect love (what the Greek calls *agape*). Accountability, encouragement, admonition, intercessory prayer, and support are impossible apart from other people. We become a holy people *together*. We hear the voice of God most clearly in community. Love is superficial until it is lived out in the context of real relationships. The journey of grace is a team event![35]

So here they are, side by side. Two distinct equations for growth in discipleship.

The *popular* equation:

Salvation + Time + Individual Willpower = Spiritual Growth

The *holiness* equation:

Grace + Cooperation with God + Christian Community = Christlikeness

Christians are called to grow in grace, which is another way to say that we are to grow into the likeness of Jesus. We receive new life from Christ so we can grow up in Christ. God remakes and remodels. It is sanctifying grace. I know of no one who says it more whimsically than C. S. Lewis:

Imagine yourself as a living house. God comes in to rebuild that house. At first, perhaps, you can understand what he is doing. He is getting the drains right and stopping the leaks in the roof and so on; you knew those jobs needed doing and so you are not surprised. But presently he starts knocking the house about in a way that hurts abominably and does not seem to make any sense.

---

35. White, *Rethinking the Church*, 61. See also chapter 5 and the emphasis on Christian accountability and sustaining grace.

What on earth is he up to? The explanation is that he is building quite a different house from the one you thought of—throwing out a new wing here, putting on an extra floor there, running up towers, making courtyards. You thought you were being made into a decent little cottage: but he is building a palace. He intends to come and live in it himself.[36]

God not only saves us, but he also transforms us. He accepts us where we are but loves us enough not to leave us there. He reimagines, remakes, and remodels. When we offer ourselves in complete consecration and full surrender to God the Father, God the Holy Spirit cleanses and purifies our hearts, remaking us into the image of God the Son. We become Christlike in our thoughts, words, and deeds. Our house is under new management.

"Holiness means there is no corner of your life shut off from the control of Jesus Christ."[37] We take our hands off the steering wheel and let Jesus call the shots and give the orders. We say, "You have been my Savior (salvation); now I bow my knee and make you my Lord (sanctification)." We are set apart for a holy purpose, and God's perfect love begins to flow through us. We begin to love God truly with all our heart, mind, and strength, and our neighbor as ourselves.

Entire Sanctification Defined

A few last words on what is meant by *entire sanctification*. "Entire" does not refer to a *completed* work of God in us, but in a very real sense, it is *completeness*. God continuously works within us and upon us, so in that sense, the masterpiece of our life is ongoing until the

---

36. C. S. Lewis, *Mere Christianity* (New York: Touchstone, 1996), 175–76.

37. I first heard Dennis Kinlaw use this phrasing in a 1991 seminary chapel sermon. It was also the first time I remember understanding that God's control of my life was not a desire for manipulation on God's part but a longing for intimacy. In my estimation, Kinlaw was one of the finest Holiness preachers of the late twentieth century and early twenty-first century, until his death in 2017.

final resurrection of all things, including our glorification.[38] We are whole and as "completely completed" by sanctifying grace as we can be in that moment. Our lives are marked by the exquisite splendor of *shalom*. *Shalom* is what God is conceiving in creation and fashioning in our lives. *Shalom* certainly means peace, but it also means wholeness, completeness, unity, and every part working in harmony with the goal (*telos*) for which we were created.

Entire sanctification, as we discussed already, is a lifetime of persistent renunciation of self-centered existence (flesh) and the continual submission of nonresistant obedience to the ways and will of God. As Jesus said with great precision: "If any want to become my followers [disciples], let them deny themselves [flesh] and take up their cross daily and follow me" (Luke 9:23).[39] The result of such a cross-centered life is Christlikeness manifesting in perfect love for God and neighbor.

The tenth Article of Faith for the Church of the Nazarene articulates sanctification thus:

We believe that entire sanctification is that act of God, subsequent to regeneration, by which believers are made free from original

---

38. "Glorification" refers to the state of a believer after death and the final resurrection of all things. "Through God's grace we shall ultimately be glorified—resurrected with Christ when he returns, and transformed into his complete likeness, to enjoy his glory forever." Greathouse and Dunning, *An Introduction to Wesleyan Theology*, 54. Additionally, Diane LeClerc refers to glorification as final sanctification in "that a person is removed from the very presence of sin." LeClerc, *Discovering Christian Holiness*, 318.

39. In reference to the idea that entire sanctification implies a lifetime of denying oneself (flesh) and taking up one's cross, "J. O. McClurkan, leader of one of the southern branches of the early Holiness Movement, referred to this latter aspect of the sanctified life as 'a deeper death to self,' which in reality should be occurring throughout the Christian life. . . . From experience, he recognized that not all of life could be compressed into one moment of experience." Dunning, *Pursuing the Divine Image*, Kindle Location 853. For further discussion of this, see William J. Strickland and H. Ray Dunning, *J. O. McClurkan: His Life, His Theology, and Selections from His Writings* (Nashville: Trevecca Press, 1998).

sin, or depravity, and brought into a state of entire devotement to God, and the holy obedience of love made perfect.

It is wrought by the baptism with or infilling of the Holy Spirit, and comprehends in one experience the cleansing of the heart from sin and the abiding, indwelling presence of the Holy Spirit, empowering the believer for life and service. Entire sanctification is provided by the blood of Jesus, is wrought instantaneously by grace through faith, preceded by entire consecration; and to this work and state of grace the Holy Spirit bears witness.

We believe that the grace of entire sanctification includes the divine impulse to grow in grace as a Christlike disciple. However, this impulse must be consciously nurtured, and careful attention given to the requisites and processes of spiritual development and improvement in Christlikeness of character and personality. Without such purposeful endeavor, one's witness may be impaired and the grace itself frustrated and ultimately lost.

Participating in the means of grace, especially the fellowship, disciplines, and sacraments of the church, believers grow in grace and in wholehearted love to God and neighbor.[40]

We must end our discussion of sanctifying grace with a simple question: For what purpose? Why is this desired holiness needed? What will be the evidence of a life marked by such Christlikeness?

We return to perfect love. Entire sanctification is not the pinnacle of morality. It is the highest form of self-giving love. Entire sanctification is holy love made complete in us. That Wesley defined entire sanctification as perfect love is well known. It was the singular content of his teaching on holiness. Mildred Bangs Wynkoop makes this point, claiming: "Wesley's discussions of any segment of Christian truth led him quickly into love. 'God is love.' Every aspect of the atonement is

---

40. Church of the Nazarene, *Manual: 2017-2021*, "X. Christian Holiness and Entire Sanctification" (Kansas City, MO: Nazarene Publishing House, 2017), 31-32.

an expression of love; holiness is love; the meaning of 'religion' is love. Christian perfection is perfection of love. Every step of God toward man, and man's response, step by step, is some aspect of love."[41] To drive home the point, Wynkoop adds, "To say that Christian holiness is our *raison d'être* [reason for being] is to say we are committed to everything love is, and that is a large order indeed."[42]

In short, love is the heart of the matter. Anything less than love does not hit the high mark set for the "reason for being" of a holy life. Any understanding of entire sanctification devoid of love is harsh, legalistic, judgmental, and unholy. *Agape* (Christian love) is the love that holds all other natural loves in their proper order.[43] *Agape* guides, interprets, and controls all other desires. Because we are encouraged to increase in *agape*, we understand that it is given and enhanced; it is both a gift and is grown in us by the abiding presence of the Holy Spirit. Effort is needed, but grace is provided.

We are drawn by holy love through seeking (prevenient) grace. We are captured by holy love through saving grace. We are purified and set apart by holy love through sanctifying grace. We grow in grace as we abound in holy love. This is how we experience the fullness of life in Christ.

---

41. Mildred Bangs Wynkoop, A *Theology of Love: The Dynamic of Wesleyanism* (Kansas City, MO: Beacon Hill Press of Kansas City, 1972), 36.

42. Wynkoop, A *Theology of Love*, 36.

43. For an enlightening summary of the four Greek terms for love—*eros, storge, philia*, and *agape*—I highly recommend Wynkoop's short exegesis under the heading "Love and Fellowship." She argues that all but *agape* are natural loves, requiring little effort. *Agape* is not only a different dimension of love, but it is also a quality by which one orders life, only made possible by the fullness of Christ. "The love which we call Christian love, then, is not a substitute for the other loves, nor is it an addition to those loves, but it is a quality of the entire person as it is centered in Christ. The distorting self-orientation, which flaws all other relationships because it uses them to personal advantage (often in most subtle and devious ways), is brought into wholeness by the abiding presence of the Holy Spirit. In this relationship all other relationships of life are enhanced and beautified and made holy." Wynkoop, A *Theology of Love*, 38.

5
SUSTAINING GRACE

*Now to him who is able to keep you from falling, and to
make you stand without blemish in the presence of his glory
with rejoicing, to the only God our Savior, through Jesus
Christ our Lord, be glory, majesty, power, and authority,
before all time and now and forever. Amen.*
—Jude 1:24–25

There comes a point in every Christian's life when something begins to dawn on them. Sometimes it happens immediately, and sometimes it happens further along the journey of grace: *aspects of my life remain un-surrendered to the lordship of Christ. There are rooms in my being-remodeled house* (to return to C. S. Lewis's illustration) *that remain closed off from God's work.*

Because God is relentlessly committed to our holiness, making us more and more like Jesus, the Holy Spirit begins to probe, "Is everything mine? Does every part of you belong to me? Is there anything you are holding back?"

Our first response may be to say, "You can have anything but (fill in the blank). I have given you 99 percent of me. Is there nothing I get to keep for myself? Do you expect *everything?*"[1]

---

1. "Beware of ever thinking, 'Oh, that thing in my life doesn't matter much.' The fact that it doesn't matter much to you may mean that it matters a great deal to God.

With patient love and unwavering dedication to fulfilling the ultimate end goal (*telos*) of our discipleship, the Spirit of Jesus whispers, "Yes, *all* of you. One hundred percent. Nothing held back."

To be wholly God's is to share in all of God's promised life. As more of our self is relinquished to God, so follows greater peace and joy. Oswald Chambers believes that eternal life is not a gift *from* God but a gift *of* God. Further, the spiritual power Jesus promised to his disciples after his resurrection and in anticipation of Pentecost is not a gift *from* the Holy Spirit, but the power *is* the Holy Spirit (Acts 1:8). The result is an endless supply of abundant life that increases with every relinquishment to God. Again, Chambers's insight is enlightening: "Even the weakest saint can experience the power of the deity of the Son of God, when he is willing to 'let go.' But any effort to 'hang on' to the least bit of our own power will only diminish the life of Jesus in us. We have to keep letting go, and slowly, but surely, the great full life of God will invade us, penetrating every part."[2]

The human heart is the locus of sin and disobedience, but it is also the locus of grace and holiness. In seeking grace, God woos our heart; in saving grace God captures our heart; in sanctifying grace, God cleanses our heart. Our predisposition moves from the heart of a servant to the heart of a child. We discover that we no longer serve God out of fear of what might happen if we didn't obey; instead, we have been given a heart of love that gives us a desire to obey. Make no mistake, however: the claim of Christ throughout the journey of grace is for nothing less than all of us—entire, complete, whole.

Holiness is to be set apart for a holy purpose and to be so filled with the Spirit of Jesus that our mindset, motives, and attitudes are

---

Nothing should be considered a trivial matter by a child of God. . . . Nothing in our lives is a mere insignificant detail to God." Oswald Chambers, My *Utmost for His Highest* (Uhrichsville, OH: Barbour and Company, 1935), 76–77.

2. Chambers, My *Utmost for His Highest*, 74–75.

Christlike. We deny ourselves, which means we give up our right to "me." We take up our cross, which means we transfer our rights to Jesus. Here is the surprising paradox: in giving up our right to "me" and transferring our rights to Jesus, we find life. When we lose our life in Christ, we find it. That which is withheld from God is finally lost; that which is released to God cannot be taken. "For you have died, and your life is hidden with Christ in God" (Col. 3:3). The consecration is total.

Our consecration to God is not the source of our sanctification. We cannot sanctify ourselves; we do not make ourselves holy. The Spirit of Jesus does this. It is not enough to *want* to be like Jesus. Desire is not enough, and imitation will only go so far. We must have the Spirit of Jesus in us, or as Paul says, Christ must be formed in you (Gal. 4:19).

In many respects, the Pharisees were the best people of Jesus's day. They were moral, they were clean, and they were good. Nevertheless, their goodness was located in behavior modification and in their attempts to be holy through a system of sin management that never dealt with their hearts. They wanted to be godly and lead pure lives, but their self-denial turned out to be self-serving, and their cross-bearing made them less loving. One can only manage the outside for so long before the inside takes over. As mentioned earlier, whatever is in your heart will eventually escape. The Pharisee Christian—one who tries to lead a holy life by self-directed effort and the flesh—will always fall short of perfect love because it is not enough to *want* to be like Jesus. The Spirit of Jesus must be in us. This is the crux of heart holiness. Grace is needed to empower, enable, and lead a holy life.

Dallas Willard explains that the holy life actually requires more grace than any attempts to imitate Jesus through self-directed undertakings: "If you would really like to be into consuming grace, just lead a holy life. The true saint burns grace like a 747 burns fuel on takeoff. Become the kind of person who routinely does what Jesus did and said. You will consume much more grace by leading a holy life than you will by sinning because every holy act you do will have to be upheld by the grace of God. And that upholding is totally the unmerited favor of God in action."[3] We must have the unremitting upholding of God's sustaining grace—the grace that keeps us from falling (Jude 1:24).

Having said that, sustaining grace does not deny the need for our participation. In chapter 4, we saw that grace means God has done everything we could not do for ourselves, but it does not mean we now become grace consumers who contribute nothing to the relationship. We cooperate with the active grace of God by reordering our lives around those activities, disciplines, and practices that Jesus modeled. We participate in them not to earn our sanctification but to accomplish through training what we cannot do by trying harder.

Imparted Righteousness

Perhaps a few words on the difference between imputed and imparted righteousness will be helpful. According to Diane LeClerc, imputed righteousness is "the righteousness of Jesus credited to the Christian, which then enables the Christian to be justified. God sees the person through Christ's righteousness, but it does not speak to the inner transformation and cleansing of the individual by God." Imparted righteousness, on the other hand, is "a gracious gift of God given at the very moment of the new birth of an individual. God begins the process of making us holy."[4]

---

3. Willard, *The Great Omission: Reclaiming Jesus's Essential Teachings On Discipleship* (New York: HarperCollins, 2006), 62.

4. Diane LeClerc, *Discovering Christian Holiness: The Heart of Wesleyan-Holiness Theology* (Kansas City, MO: Beacon Hill Press of Kansas City, 2010), 312. This is also why John Wesley referred to the new birth as initial sanctification. While not denying

The difference between the two is not as subtle as you may think. One is a credited righteousness—applied, as it were; the other is a given righteousness that indwells. Imparted righteousness can be understood as the gift of God that enables and empowers a disciple of Christ to strive for holiness, sanctification, and perfect love. More precisely, Timothy Tennent captures the difference well: "As Christians, we know that God takes sinners and clothes them with the righteousness of Christ (imputed). God then works in us every good work, so that the righteousness that was once merely imputed to us becomes, in real time, imparted to us, in ever-increasing measures."[5]

Optimism of Grace

Imparted righteousness is what made John Wesley so thoroughly optimistic about the potential of transformation. Fully recognizing the devastation of original sin, Wesley was not optimistic about human nature. However, he was utterly convinced that God's grace could literally transform a life from the inside out.

I once heard my friend Wesley Tracy refer to it as the "radical optimism of grace." To illustrate, he told me a story: Imagine there is a little girl who walks into the back of the church. She is eleven or twelve. Her clothes are dirty and unkempt; her hair is thin and matted down. She smells musty, as if she has not had a real bath in more than a few days. You know a little of her history. School is not going well. She is falling behind in her classes and not making passing grades. You are fairly certain the problem isn't her intellect but,

---

the other, the Reformed tradition tends to put the emphasis on imputed righteousness, while Wesleyan-Holiness theology puts the primary emphasis on imparted righteousness.

5. Timothy Tennent, "Living in a Righteousness Orientation: Psalm 26" *Seedbed Daily Text*, September 1, 2019, https://www.seedbed.com/living-in-a-righteousness-orientation-psalm-26/. Tennent adds: "Only in the new creation is this made fully complete, but sanctification is the call of every believer—to be set apart as holy—so that with full hearts, we can praise the Lord 'in the great assembly' (Psalm 26:12)."

more likely, what is going on at home. She doesn't know her biological father, and her mother has had several live-in boyfriends. There are rumors of child abuse behind closed doors, and the bruises on her arms seem to confirm it.

Tracy then said, "A behaviorist would look at that young girl and say, 'She is scarred for life; forever messed up. Some things are salvageable, but she will always walk with a limp, and she can never be all she could have been if her environment had been different.' That's what a behaviorist would say." But, Tracy continues, "Do you know what someone who believes in the radical optimism of grace would say? 'No matter what has been done to her or what she does to herself, that little girl has the hope of the gospel. God can take her where she is and make her what he wants her to be.'" Or, as Wesley might put it, "Show me the vilest wretch in all of London, and I will show you someone who has all the grace of the apostles themselves."

This optimism takes seriously our sinful condition, but it takes even more seriously the power of grace to take anyone, from anywhere, from anything, and make him or her all God wants them to be.[6] No pain is so painful, no hurt is so hurtful, no wound is so deep, no sin is so awful that God's grace cannot transform, heal, and make whole again.

Pardon and Power

The journey of grace is the transformation of the whole person. Righteousness is imparted; holiness is given. It is not "try harder" or "get yourself together," but a true change that results in empowered living. Put differently, God's grace is needed for pardon and power. We need forgiveness of our sins (pardon), and we need strength

---

6. "As Wesley would say, to deny such optimism would make the power of sin greater than the power of grace—an option that should be unthinkable for a Wesleyan-Holiness theology." LeClerc, *Discovering Christian Holiness*, 27.

(power) to live a life that honors God. One without the other leads to dangerous extremes. If we say God will forgive us but doesn't really care how we live our imperfect lives because, after all, it is all covered by grace, we are in danger of antinomianism. Conversely, if we assume grace is only needed to pardon our sins but then it is up to us to take it from there, we are in danger of legalism. Both are dangerous extremes that are impediments to the journey of grace. The apostle Paul speaks to these two extremes when he says, "Work out your own salvation with fear and trembling; for it is God who is at work in you, enabling you both to will and to work for his good pleasure" (Phil. 2:12–13). Who is responsible for our spiritual growth? Is it our job or God's job? Paul's answer is yes to both, and that is not a contradiction.

Consider the extreme of legalism. Legalism in its strictest theological definition is the overemphasized notion that obedience to rules, regulations and particular codes of conduct is necessary for salvation. Practically speaking, legalism says, we know that God has provided for our salvation through the cross of Jesus, but whether it is ever actualized in our life is dependent on whether we pray a lot, read our Bible every day, and are careful to avoid certain people and places. At its heart, legalism is trying to do for ourselves what only God can do. The result of a person bent on keeping the rules is an enormous amount of guilt, fear, frustration, and insecurity with very little grace, peace, or assurance. It is grace-less discipleship and, taken to its furthest extreme, becomes an elusive form of self-righteous humanism and an air of superiority. Legalists have high expectations for themselves but even higher standards for everyone else, which is unattractive and repels those who are alienated from the church.

In contrast to legalism is the opposite extreme of antinomianism. Antinomianism is a technical word that derives from two Greek words: *anti*, meaning "against," and *nomos*, meaning "law." Combined, it expresses the idea of lawlessness. While it is true—and we have spent a great deal of time arguing this point—that a Christian is saved by grace alone and not by good works or our own actions, this truth does not free us from moral and spiritual obligations. Practically speaking, the antinomian person says, "Since grace abounds why not sin all the more so that I receive even more grace? Because I am covered by grace, I am under no obligation to obey any ethical or moral standard. I have been freed from the burden of responsibility. Love covers all." As illogical (and impractical) as that may sound, it is the mindset of some Christians. "Don't ask me for any serious commitment or self-sacrifice. I am done with laying a heavy spiritual burden on anyone's shoulders because that just leads to old-fashioned guilt and legalism. I am into grace."[7] Notably, though John Wesley was no legalist, he believed the antinomian way of thinking to be an even greater danger than legalism and considered antinomianism the worst of all heresies because it devalued perfect love. Love without holiness is permissive; holiness without love is harsh.

In 1751, John Wesley wrote a letter to a friend, most believe, in response to accusations that his preaching was either too legalistic or too permissive (antinomian). His response was instructive: "I would not advise to preach the law without the gospel any more than the gospel without the law. Undoubtedly, both should be preached in their turns; yea, both at once, or both in one." Wesley sums up what he means by "both in one" held in tension: "God loves you; therefore love and obey him. Christ died for you; therefore die to sin. Christ is risen; therefore rise in the image of God. Christ liveth evermore; therefore live to God till you live with him in glory. . . . This is the

---

7. In a conversation with Wesley scholar Dr. Cliff Sanders regarding legalism and antinomianism, Sanders made an interesting point: "Fifty years ago legalism was the greater challenge for evangelical churches. Today it is more likely antinomianism, as the particular struggle of many young adults who have been raised in the church and want to leave the holy out of love."

Scriptural way, the Methodist way, the true way. God grant we may never turn therefrom, to the right hand or to the left.[8]

So which is it? Are our salvation and spiritual growth God's job or our job? Paul makes it clear: it is not either/or but both/and. Full salvation is God's work from start to finish. We are sought, saved, sanctified, and sustained by God's grace. But we are also admonished again and again to make every effort to cooperate with the Holy Spirit's work in our lives (Luke 13:24; Phil. 2:12–13; 2 Tim. 2:15; Heb. 12:14; 2 Pet. 1:5–7; 3:13–34).[9]

Grace is for both pardon and power. This is how sustaining grace contributes to our discipleship in the divine-human partnership. God initiates, we respond. God calls, we listen. God guides, we obey. God empowers, we work. "For first, God works; therefore you can work," Wesley said. "Secondly, God works; therefore you must work."[10]

The Necessity of Free Will

The subject of this chapter is sustaining grace—or, that grace which enables us to do what God calls us to do and to live holy lives. The New Testament book of Jude refers to this grace, in the benediction, as the power of God that keeps us from falling and causes us to stand blameless before him on the final day. Such a declaration communicates a very important truth about our discipleship: we can fall from grace, but the sustaining grace of God makes it possible not to have to.

There once was a time when a few well-intentioned Holiness preachers said that once you are sanctified you would never sin again.

---

8. John Wesley, "Letter on Preaching Christ," *The Works of the Rev. John Wesley*, Volume 6.

9. See chapter 2's emphasis on "working out in the world what God is working in us."

10. John Wesley, "Sermon 85: On Working Out Our Own Salvation," III.2, http://wesley.nnu.edu/john-wesley/the-sermons-of-john-wesley-1872-edition/sermon-85-on-working-out-our-own-salvation/.

This proclamation generated much confusion and consternation among sincere Christians who were passionate about their walk with Christ but who discovered that not only was it possible to stumble and fall, but that it was done with some frequency, especially in light of messages that told them entire sanctification would remedy the problem. That simply is not the case—the reason being that our free will is never taken out of the equation. Free will remains forever in the life of a believer because it is based in the necessity of relationship. Love is relational, and choice is a necessary component of any healthy relationship. In fact, the image of God is stamped on us, and that which is being restored in the *fullness* of Christ is the capacity for holy and loving relationships.

The creation account in Genesis is illuminating. A sovereign God speaks the universe into existence with little more effort than spoken words: "Let there be . . . ". God's rule is absolute and his dominion unparalleled—yet, astonishingly, human freedom is interwoven into the fabric of creation. Given God's unrivaled power to create and sustain, this freedom is unexpected because, as we later learn, the distinct choices of human beings are not only permitted, but they also have the potential to help or harm the flourishing of God's good world. The all-powerful One, at great risk, allows our choices to matter.

In the first paradise, "the LORD God commanded the man, 'You may freely eat of every tree of the garden; but of the tree of the knowledge of good and evil you shall not eat, for in the day that you eat it you shall die'" (Gen. 2:16–17). The power to choose was given in the command. At first, one might think this unfair of God. Why would God command something knowing that the moment you tell someone what he or she cannot do, it is all they can think about? Was this a setup for temptation? No: God did not tempt them. They were given a choice. The two are not the same. In the command is a recognition of free will (or freed will).[11] Freed will is necessary for love to exist in a relationship.

If my wife was *forced* to love me and had no choice in the matter, we would still have a relationship, more or less, but it would not be a marriage. Why? Because, if I were in full control, it would become something other than love. She would become an automaton, a robot who could not voluntarily act any other way. The only way we can share a healthy marriage is if we are both given the choice to love the other. Therein lies the inherent risk of love: she could choose not to love me.

When God made human beings, he placed them in a beautiful garden filled with life and goodness. It was pure grace in that it was initiated and provided by God with no contribution on their part. But God did not make them robots who had to do his will. They could choose between good or evil. They had the choice to love God, or not. Almost as if God were saying, "Do this one thing because I am God. Your obedience is a choice. I want this relationship to be based on love, not control." God gives us a free will not because he wants to tempt us but because he wants us to choose him back. Only then will it be a volitional relationship rooted in love.

Søren Kierkegaard believed a surrendered will to be the sign of a heart made pure: "Purity of heart is to *will* one thing." The opposite of a pure heart is double-mindedness, also reflected in the will. The answer to whether the entirely sanctified can ever sin again is yes. It is possible to fall from grace because one is always free to respond to God or the temptation at hand. For the sake of love, the choice will always be our

---

11. Mildred Bangs Wynkoop reminds us that John Wesley's primary emphasis was more on free grace than free will. Therefore, those in the Wesleyan tradition would more accurately speak of "freed will," which refers to the will empowered and set free by the Holy Spirit, making it possible for a person actively to confess faith in Jesus Christ. All the way through, salvation is of God, by grace alone. Wynkoop, *Foundations of Wesleyan-Arminian Theology* (Kansas City, MO: Beacon Hill Press of Kansas City, 1967), 69.

own. Yet here is the major difference of a life sustained by grace: now we have the power not to have to sin. Through the power of sustaining grace, we can say yes to God and no to temptation. Our faith is protected by the power of God, shielded by a living hope through the resurrection of Jesus Christ from the dead (1 Pet. 1:3–4).

In a forthright confession, Paul admits that, before the Spirit, sin was in control of his life so strongly it was like a taskmaster to a slave. "For I do not do the good I want, but the evil I do not want is what I do" (Rom. 7:19). He was trapped in the vicious cycle of not wanting to do something but being unable to resist, and of wanting to do something but being unable to carry it out. "Who will rescue me from this body of death?" (7:24). Now that he is under the power of the Holy Spirit, Paul continues, he can say yes to God and no to temptation. "Thanks be to God through Jesus Christ our Lord! For the law of the Spirit of life in Christ Jesus has set you free from the law of sin and of death" (7:25a; 8:2). Apart from the Holy Spirit, our human will is weak and powerless to obey; with the Holy Spirit, we are empowered to obey. It is not that the sanctified can never sin again, but now we have the power not to sin. The difference is the sustaining grace of God that keeps us from falling.

Faithfulness is grounded in faith and fullness. As Wesley was quick to add, the Holy Spirit strengthens our will, that we might produce "every good desire, whether related to our tempers, words, or actions, to inward and outward holiness."[12]

Sustaining Grace as the Transformation of Character

In his immensely helpful and comprehensive book on discipleship, *After You Believe*, N. T. Wright sets forth how Christlike character is formed in persons and churches. He refers to it as the long yet steady growth in grace that comes as a result of spiritual practices

---

12. Wesley, "Sermon 85: On Working Out Our Own Salvation," III.2.

and habits formed in a person's life, that transforms them more and more into the image of Jesus Christ. The ancient writers called such character formation "virtue."

Wright begins the book by retelling the true story of Captain Chesley Sullenberger, better known as "Sully." It was a Thursday afternoon, January 15, 2009, and felt like any other day in New York City. The commercial jet took off at 3:26 p.m. bound for Charlotte. Sully was the captain. He did all the routine checks, and everything seemed normal until, just two minutes after takeoff, the airplane slammed into a flock of Canadian geese. Both engines were severely damaged and lost power. The plane was heading north over the Bronx, one of the most densely populated parts of the city. Sully and his copilot had to make major decisions, and fast. The lives of more than 150 passengers, and thousands more on the ground, were at stake.

The closest smaller airports were too far away, and landing on the New Jersey Turnpike would have been a disaster. That left them only one other option: landing on the Hudson River. In just three minutes before landing, Sully and his copilot had to do some vital things to keep from crashing. (Wright mentions nine technical and differing tasks). Remarkably, they did it; they landed the airplane on the Hudson River. Everyone got off safely, with Captain Sully walking up and down the aisle several times to check that everyone had escaped before disembarking himself.[13]

Many people said it was a miracle, and at a certain level, it surely was. Yet *where* was the miracle? For miracles come in many different forms. Was the miracle in God's supernaturally protecting and guiding hand? It is certainly possible. However, there is another way to look at it. Perhaps the miracle was Sully's virtue that made him able to respond with such technical speed under intense pressure. If using

---

13. N. T. Wright, *After You Believe: Why Christian Character Matters* (New York: HarperCollins, 2010), 18–20.

virtue in this way seems odd, it is because virtue is not just another way to say "good" or "moral." Wright argues that virtue, in the strictest sense of the word, "is what happens when someone has made a thousand small choices, requiring effort and concentration, to do something which is good and right but which doesn't 'come naturally'—and then, on the thousand and first time, when it really matters, they find that they do what's required 'automatically,' as we say."[14]

In other words, when something looks like it "just happens," we begin to realize that it didn't "just happen." As Wright points out, if any of us had been flying the airplane that day, and had only done what comes naturally, we would have crashed into the side of a skyscraper. Virtue, character formation—or, for our purposes, discipleship—that grows in grace to become more and more like Jesus is not what happens naturally; it is also what happens when wise and judicious choices become second nature. Sully wasn't born being able to fly a commercial jet, nor was he born with the character traits that were laid bare in brief moments of time—like courage, a steady hand, quick judgment, and concern for the safety of others at the risk of his own. These are acquired skills and traits that require specific practice and repetition over time—until what starts out feeling awkward begins to feel normal, and then what feels normal begins to be so ingrained into our minds and muscle memory that we react rather than having to think. It is second nature.

Not to offend any readers who may be pilots, but if I had been a passenger on that fast-descending airplane, I wouldn't want a rookie pilot just doing what came naturally. If they had to get out the engine manual, check the internet, or reach into their mental hard drive to recover what they learned in flight school for such an emergency before they could respond to a crisis they had never faced before, the

---

14. Wright, *After You Believe*, 20.

outcome could have been much different. Knowledge is not enough; nor is grit and determination. No, Wright emphatically insists, what was needed in that crisis moment was the practiced virtue of something that had become second nature—a transformation of character, "formed by the specific strengths, that is, 'virtues,' of knowing exactly how to fly a plane."[15] I would add *that* plane—the plane Sully had been trained to know intimately in every detail.

The idea of "second nature" captures my attention, especially pertaining to discipleship, holiness, and the journey of grace. Few would disagree that qualities such as courage, endurance, restraint, wisdom, good judgment, and patience do not come naturally to us. They are things that are learned and ingrained into our character, sometimes through painful and difficult circumstances but always through the filter of learned behaviors. A well-established character, attributed to in the New Testament, and as defined by Wright, is "the pattern of thinking and acting which runs right through someone, so that wherever you cut into them (as it were), you see the same person through and through."[16]

The opposite, of course, is superficiality. Many people can present themselves initially as honest, kind, positive, and the like, but the more you get to know them, the more their true colors show up and you realize they are just putting up a good front. "When faced with a crisis, or simply when their guard is down, they're as dishonest, grouchy, and impatient as the next person."[17] What is the problem? They are just doing what comes naturally; they are self-aware enough to know that their attitude should be different, but they have not acquired new second-nature habits to react well to sudden challenges and disappointments. One's character is not *made* in a crisis; it is

15. Wright, *After You Believe*, 21.
16. Wright, *After You Believe*, 27.
17. Wright, *After You Believe*, 27.

revealed. When we don't have time to think, who we really are is exposed every time.

H. Ray Dunning has shown how some of Wesley's eighteenth-century terms differ from contemporary usage. For example, as it pertains to our discussion on free will, "liberty" was the term he used for freedom of choice, whereas "will" was the term he used to refer to what he called "affections," or the inclinations that motivate human action. Affections did not refer to feelings that come and go, nor were they changed by temporary behavior modifications. They had more to do with the deeper level of why a person chooses certain choices or actions. Closely related to affections was Wesley's use of the term "temper." A temper in the eighteenth century did not mean that a person was irritable or became angry easily. Rather, it was more in line with how we use "temperament" today. Wesley used temper in the sense of "an enduring or habitual disposition of a person."[18] Or more exactly, those human affections that are focused on and developed into enduring aspects of one's character, cultivated by the means of grace, until they are no longer momentary goings-on but become long-term and stable virtues and, when done with righteous intent, "holy tempers."

"Holy tempers" was a frequently utilized phrase in Wesley's teaching on discipleship, especially in his reflections on the fruit of the Spirit in Galatians. "By contrast, the fruit of the Spirit is love, joy, peace, patience, kindness, generosity, faithfulness, gentleness, and self-control" (Gal. 5:22–23). Several facets of this text are worth highlighting. For one, Wesley was quick to mention that the fruit was singular, not plural ("fruits"). If they were plural, one might be tempted to focus on one fruit over another, as if faithfulness could be focused on and generosity ignored. The fruit as a unified whole is

---

18. Randy Maddox, *Responsible Grace: John Wesley's Practical Theology* (Nashville: Kingswood, 1994), 69.

evidence that the Spirit of God is at work. They are not independent characteristics. Then, as we grow, all nine varieties of fruit work together to paint a compelling picture of what it looks like when the Holy Spirit is in control of a consecrated life. "Paul," N. T. Wright points out, "does not envisage specialization."[19] Just as one can identify a peach tree by the fruit it produces, so a Christian is known by the fruit of the Spirit—holy tempers that are evidenced in one's life. Not surprisingly, Wesley hastened to add that love begins the list of holy tempers because all nine are expressions of love. Nevertheless, along the journey of grace, all of the characteristics of Christ will be manifested in our lives.

Perhaps most important to understand for the journey of grace is that these holy tempers are not experienced instantaneously. Instead, as Randy Maddox explains, "God's regenerating (saving) grace awakens in believers the 'seeds' of such virtues. These seeds then strengthen and take shape as we 'grow in grace.' Given liberty, this growth involves responsible cooperation, for we could instead neglect or stifle God's gracious empowerment."[20] There is so much to unpack from Maddox's explanation. But here is the primary idea that we must not miss: virtue must be nurtured to increase.

By God's grace, we are saved and sanctified in a moment of time, and we are enabled to begin the journey toward Christlikeness—the seeds of righteousness are planted. In a breathtaking undertaking of grace, we are given the freedom to leave a life of sin and self-interest so that we might love God with all our heart, soul, strength, and mind. But the three abiding virtues of faith, hope, and love (1 Cor. 13:13) and the ninefold variety of fruit proceeding from the Spirit-filled life are both *gifted* and *grown*. The fruit of the Spirit does not suddenly

---

19. Wright, *After You Believe*, 195.

20. Randy Maddox, "Reconnecting the Means to the End: A Wesleyan Prescription for the Holiness Movement," *Wesleyan Theological Journal*, vol. 33, No. 2 (Fall 1998), 41.

appear, nor does it, as Wright correctly states, "grow automatically." There are undoubtedly initial promising indications that the fruit is on the way. "Many new Christians, particularly when a sudden conversion has meant a dramatic turning away from a lifestyle full of the 'works of the flesh,' report their own astonishment at the desire that springs up within them to love, to forgive, to be gentle, to be pure. Where, they ask, has all this come from? I didn't used to be like this. That is a wonderful thing, a sure sign of the Spirit's working."[21]

These incredible "affection" changes are nothing short of a pure gift of grace. However, the new Christian cannot become passive. They have to work out what God is working in them. The same grace that made these "affection" changes possible must now be grown into "holy tempers," cultivated through new habits and acquired practices. Again, Wright precisely makes this point with a keen discipleship imagination: "These [new desires] are the blossoms; to get the fruit you have to learn to be a gardener. You have to discover how to tend and prune, how to irrigate the field, how to keep the birds and squirrels away. You have to watch for blight and mold, cut away ivy and other parasites that suck the life out of the tree, and make sure the young trunk can stand firm in strong winds. Only then will the fruit appear."[22]

The blossoms are certainly the sign of "Christ in you, the hope of glory" (Col. 1:27), but to get the actual fruit of a mature, Christlike character, we must become gardeners. The seeds must now begin to bear the fruit. Surrendered affections produce holy tempers, a new disposition, which yields Christlike thinking, and actions that begin to function in second-nature ways.[23] "My Father is glorified by this,

---

21. Wright, *After You Believe*, 195–96.

22. Wright, *After You Believe*, 196.

23. "Wesley's language of holy actions 'flowing' from holy tempers suggests that he appreciated the sense in which habituated affections bring 'freedom' for human actions—the freedom that comes from disciplined practice (e.g., the freedom to play a Bach concerto)." Maddox, *Responsible Grace*, 69.

that you bear much fruit and become my disciples" (John 15:8). The blossoms become fruit—the seeds become virtue. The energizing power of God becomes the grace that sustains.

Vice and Virtue

Paul admonishes the Corinthian Christians: "Examine yourselves to see whether you are living in the faith. Test yourselves. Do you not realize that Jesus Christ is in you?" (2 Cor. 13:5). In his customary perceptive style, Eugene Peterson's paraphrase is apropos: "Test yourselves to make sure you are solid in the faith. Don't drift along taking everything for granted. Give yourselves regular checkups. You need firsthand evidence, not mere hearsay, that Jesus Christ is in you. Test it out. If you fail the test, do something about it" (vv. 5–9, MSG).

Regular health checkups are always better than heart attacks or strokes. A problem that is found early enough is often treatable. Throughout biblical history, forty-day periods have been recognized as times of preparation, purification, and taking spiritual inventory.[24] One could make the case that the purpose of revivals and camp meetings in the Holiness tradition is for corporate and personal checkups. As referenced by Paul to the Corinthians, spiritual growth requires spiritual health. In the spirit of Paul's counsel, Wesley's belief in small accountability groups ("class meetings" as he called them) was to practice the discipline of spiritual health checkups.

What are the warning signs of spiritual heart disease? Classified by the church in the sixth century, the warning signs were identified as the "deadly sins" or "deadly vices." Just as high cholesterol is a warning for heart disease, so these signs are indicators of unhealthy tendencies in our discipleship and, unless they are dealt with, can lead to spiritual death. Though often presented as the seven deadly

---

24. The season of Lent in the Christian calendar is based on the forty-day concept of self-examination.

sins in popular culture, the church's historical understanding of vice is more comprehensive and includes the following:

Pride: putting self in the place of God as the center and main objective of one's life; refusal to recognize one's station as creature, dependent on God.

Irreverence: deliberate neglect of the worship of God, or contentment with perfunctory participation in it; manifested cynicism toward the holy or use of Christianity for the sake of personal advantage.

Sentimentality: satisfaction with pious feelings and beautiful ceremony without striving for personal holiness; no interest in bearing one's cross or personal sacrifice; a greater attraction to emotional spirituality than sacrificial commitments.

Distrust: refusal to recognize God's wisdom and love; undue worry, anxiety, scrupulosity, or perfectionism; attempts to gain or keep control of one's life by spiritualism, undue timidity, or cowardice.

Disobedience: rejection of God's known will; refusal to learn God's nature as revealed in Holy Scripture; breaking confidence by irresponsibility, treachery, and the unnecessary disappointment of others; breaking legal or moral contracts.

Impenitence: refusal to search out and face up to one's sins, or to confess them before God; self-justification by believing one's sins to be insignificant, natural, or inevitable; refusing to apologize and reconcile with one's neighbor or being unwilling to forgive oneself.

Vanity: failure to credit God and others for their contribution to one's life; boasting, exaggeration, and ostentatious behavior; undue concern over "things."

Arrogance: being overbearing and argumentative; being opinionated and obstinate.

Resentment: rejection of talents, abilities, or opportunities God and others offer for our well-being; rebellion and hatred of God or others; cynicism.

Envy: dissatisfaction with our place in God's order of creation; manifests in jealousy, malice, and contempt for others or others' "things."

Covetousness: the refusal to respect the integrity of other creatures, expressed in the accumulation of material things to prove self-worth; the use of others to personal advantage; the quest for status and power at the expense of others.

Greed: the waste of natural resources or personal possessions; extravagance or living beyond one's means; manifests in inordinate ambition or domination of others and undue protection of one's "things"; stinginess; avarice.

Gluttony: overindulgence of natural appetites for food and drink; the inordinate quest for pleasure and comfort; manifests in intemperance and lack of discipline.

Lust: misuse of sex; includes unchastity, immodesty, prudery, and cruelty; does not recognize marriage as the God-ordained relationship for sexuality.

Sloth: the refusal to respond to one's opportunities for growth, service, and sacrifice; includes laziness in spiritual, mental, or physical duties; neglect of family; indifference to injustice or to the world's suffering people; neglecting the needy, lonely, and unpopular.

The warning signs can be subtle but hazardous to the soul. When we want to get physically healthy, we change certain lifestyle patterns and make food choices relative to our new desires—occasionally medication is needed to supplement or offset what our bodies cannot produce on their own. The truth is, our bodies do better when a quick fix is not required. Regular and ongoing attention is preferred. The life of discipleship functions in the same way. Admittedly, one cannot simply get rid of certain unhealthy patterns without replacing them with something else, something better. There must be a displacing good that is stronger than the current bad. Anyone on the road to addiction recovery will tell you that something must replace the dependency. There must be a higher, spiritual passion to displace the lower, sinful one. Likewise, there must be a regular maintenance program to enhance our journey of grace—a regular, systematic way of keeping our discipleship at peak performance levels.

What is the displacing good that replaces the deadly vices? What is the sustaining grace maintenance plan? The New Testament identifies the displacing good as the fruit of the Spirit—those life-giving virtues that displace the lower instincts of our flesh. The regular, systematic maintenance plan is called spiritual disciplines. Professional athletes run laps, stretch, and lift weights—not for fun or because they are bored but because they are determined to accomplish a goal. Spiritual checkups do not have to be major or invasive surgery. They can be wellness checks. The medicine of the displacing good is the fruit of the Spirit; the health maintenance plan to enhance our receptivity to the activity of God is the spiritual disciplines. They are essential elements of sustaining grace.

Discipline as a Means of Grace

The writer to the Hebrews recognizes the importance of spiritual discipline: "Now, discipline always seems painful rather than pleasant at the time, but later it yields the peaceful fruit of righteousness to those who have been trained by it" (12:11). Discipline can have a negative connotation, if viewed as punishment for wrongdoing. But, as Hebrews acknowledges, there is also such a thing as discipline to protect or make stronger. This is the aspect of discipline that Hebrews is referring to. "Endure trials for the sake of discipline. God is treating you as children; for what child is there whom a parent does not discipline? If you do not have that discipline in which all children share, then you are illegitimate and not his children" (vv. 7–8).

Two things of note: (1) the writer could not imagine children who are not the beneficiaries of parental discipline; (2) the writer envisions discipline as a form of holy love. To love a child includes discipline. It is not punishing a child to deny them pizza at midnight, to establish a curfew, or to refuse free rein to watch whatever they choose on Netflix. The wise parent knows this is not punishment; this is preparation for their future. It may feel unfair to the child, even cruel, but there comes a day when they learn to appreciate the boundaries set by loving parents to protect them and help them develop into fully functioning, healthy adults. In similar ways, God disciplines us toward holiness. It may not seem pleasant at the time, but it plants seeds for the peaceful fruit of a righteous life, and—do not miss this—we have to be *trained* in it.

E. Stanley Jones wisely said: "You cannot *attain* salvation by disciplines—it is the gift of God. But you cannot *retain* it without disciplines."[25] Concerning character formation, Augustine is credited with defining virtue as "a good habit consonant with our nature." Further, Jones cites the simple habits of Jesus as an example of one who was utterly dependent upon God and personally disciplined in his habits: "He did three things by habit: (1) 'He stood up to read as was his custom'—he read the Word of God by habit. (2) 'He went out into the mountain to pray as was his custom'—he prayed by habit. (3) 'He taught them again as was his custom'—he passed on to others by habit what he had and what he had found. These simple habits

---

25. E. Stanley Jones, *Conversion* (Nashville: Abingdon Press, 1991), quoted in Richard J. Foster and James Bryan Smith, eds., *Devotional Classics: Selected Readings for Individuals and Groups* (Englewood, CO: Renovaré, 1990), 281.

were the foundation habits of his life."[26] Holy habits form healthy disciples.

Returning to Wesley's thinking, he believed that holy tempers were formed in Christians as they participated in the life of the church through habitual practices he called the means of grace— also known as spiritual disciplines. Means of grace are conduits of God's transforming grace—those activities that channel the activity of God to us in the journey of grace.

For Wesley, these means were conveyed through what he called works of piety and works of mercy. Works of piety are primarily what we do to enhance our personal relationship with Christ. Works of mercy are connected to what we do to engage God's ministry and mission in the world. Both works of piety and works of mercy have an individual component (what one can do alone) and a communal component (what must be done with the help of others).

Individual works of piety include meditating on the scriptures, prayer, fasting, sharing faith with others (evangelism), and giving generously of our resources. Communal works of piety include shared worship, participating in the sacraments of Holy Communion and Christian baptism, accountability to one another (also known as Christian conferencing), Bible study, and preaching. Once again, we perform these religious events not merely because we are Christians but also because they are "Spirit-infused practices that will reform and retrain your loves . . . counterformative practices, with hunger-shaping rituals and love-shaping liturgies" because through these practices we learn to put on Christ (see Col. 3:12–16).[27]

---

26. Jones, *Conversion*, quoted in Foster and Smith, *Devotional Classics*, 282.

27. James K. A. Smith, *You Are What You Love: The Spiritual Power of Habit* (Grand Rapids: Brazos Press, 2016), 68–69.

Sacraments as Means of Grace

More detail on the importance of the sacraments will be helpful to the journey of grace. The word "sacrament" originates from
a Latin word that means "to hallow, consecrate" or "make sacred,
holy," which in turn is derived from the Greek word for "mystery."
When aligned together, a sacrament is "a sacred mystery." John Wesley borrowed his definition of a sacrament given in the catechism
of the Anglican Book of Prayer (which borrowed from Augustine's
succinct definition), with a slight adaption for greater clarity: "An
outward sign of an inward grace, and a *means* whereby we receive
the same."[28] Combining the idea of sacred mystery and means,
N. T. Wright describes sacraments as "those occasions when the
life of heaven intersects mysteriously with the life of earth."[29] Some
Christian traditions observe more sacraments than others do. Prot-
estants commonly advocate for two: baptism and the Eucharist (also
called the Lord's Supper or Holy Communion).[30]

John Wesley strongly encouraged "a close attendance on all the
ordinances (spiritual disciplines),"[31] but especially to the Eucharist.
He referred to it as "the grand channel" whereby grace is conveyed to
us, and even identified partaking of Communion as the first step in
working out our salvation.[32] Such a dynamic viewpoint was based on
his belief that Communion is more than a symbolic remembrance of
Christ's death but that the real presence of Christ, by the Holy Spirit,

---

28. Rob L. Staples, *Outward Sign and Inward Grace: The Place of Sacraments in Wesleyan Spirituality* (Kansas City, MO: Beacon Hill Press of Kansas City, 1991), 21. Emphasis added.

29. Wright, *After You Believe*, 223.

30. The rationale for two sacraments is a preference for practicing only those instituted by Jesus Christ (also known as "dominical sacraments").

31. John Wesley, *A Plain Account of Christian Perfection, Annotated*, eds. Randy L. Maddox and Paul W. Chilcote (Kansas City, MO: Beacon Hill Press of Kansas City, 2015), 45.

32. Maddox, *Responsible Grace*, 202.

is experienced when one receives the Lord's Supper.[33] This led Wesley to draw two considerable conclusions. First, because present grace is extended for empowered Christian living, Communion should be received as often as possible. Second, because the presence of the Holy Spirit in Communion is the equivalent of God's readily available saving, sanctifying, and sustaining grace, it could be considered a "converting ordinance"[34]—a person with a repentant heart could be saved—and as a means for the promotion of holiness. This high view of Communion prompted Nazarene theologian Rob Staples to refer to the Eucharist as the "sacrament of sanctification."[35]

Baptism is much more than a simple ritual or public testimony. It signifies our dying and rising with Christ. "Therefore we have been buried with him by baptism into death, so that, just as Christ was raised from the dead by the glory of the Father, so we too might walk in newness of life" (Rom. 6:4). One does not drift into the kingdom of God—eventually, there must be a dying to sin and self and a rising to new life.[36] Baptism marks that moment. "Baptism makes it crystal clear that all Christian life is a matter of being signed with the cross, of sharing in the cross, of taking up the cross and following Jesus."[37] Wesley did not include baptism in any of his formal inventories of the

---

33. "When Jesus says 'remembrance,' the Greek word is *anamnesis*. It is far more than historical recollection. It points to a Holy Spirit-inspired remembrance that ushers the event from the past into the present in such a way it is literally 'happening again.'" J. D. Walt, "Wonder Bread," *Seedbed Daily Text*, April 24, 2020, https://www.seedbed.com/wilderness-wonder-bread/.

34. "Converting ordinance" is a phrase John Wesley personally used. Staples, *Outward Sign and Inward Grace*, 252. From his own mother's testimony that she was given full assurance of her faith while partaking of Communion, and many other testimonies of experiences such as this, Wesley became convinced that the Eucharistic moment "'re-presents' Christ's once-for-all sacrifice in a dramatic display, conveying its salvific power." Maddox, *Responsible Grace*, 203.

35. See Staples, *Outward Sign and Inward Grace*, 201–49.

36. Wright, *After You Believe*, 281.

37. Wright, *After You Believe*, 281.

means of grace, not because he devalued baptism but because of its initiatory role into the community of faith and as a single event in the life of a believer. Thus, for Wesley, baptism marked the initiation of the life of holiness, while Wesley saw the other means of grace as necessarily repeated for the ongoing pursuit of holiness.[38]

Wesley was very much aligned with the English Reformers on much of his baptismal view, but he differed in two substantial ways. According to Maddox, Wesley exalted "the graciously empowered transformation of our lives" over the conferring of our "juridical pardon (a focus on guilt and the necessity of forgiveness)." This is an important distinction because it means that baptism is not only a sign that our sins are forgiven but also that we are being healed of our sinful nature and the brokenness sin has inflicted on us.[39] Additionally, for Wesley, though the grace of baptism is "sufficient for initiating Christian life," one must participate *responsively* and *responsibly* with the grace that is given for the means of grace to be fully efficient.[40] In this sense, baptism is a sign and symbol of one's willingness to engage fully in what is needed to nurture a holy life.

Nazarene historian and scholar Paul Bassett once told me that the earliest recorded baptismal liturgy, from the late fourth century, included the officiant's laying on of hands and saying of the words (my paraphrase): "And now receive the grace and healing of our Lord Jesus Christ, and may the power of the Holy Spirit work within you, that

---

38. Staples, *Outward Sign and Inward Grace*, 98; Maddox, *Responsible Grace*, 222.

39. There are significant differences between Western (Latin) and Eastern (Greek) Christian traditions in regard to the meaning of salvation. "Western Christianity (both Protestant and Catholic) came to be characterized by a dominant *juridical* emphasis on guilt and absolution, while Eastern Orthodox soteriology typically emphasized more the *therapeutic* concern for healing our sin-diseased nature." Maddox, *Responsible Grace*, 23. Wesley's view of the meaning of baptism included both but emphasized the healing and life-giving aspect.

40. Maddox, *Responsible Grace*, 23.

being born of water and the Spirit you may be a faithful witness." In short, *I have received grace; I am being healed; I will be a disciple of Jesus.*

Accountable Relationships

Any discussion of sustaining grace in the life of discipleship would be incomplete, especially for those in the Wesleyan-Holiness tradition, without a mention of the importance of spiritually accountable relationships. Wesley developed a practical framework he believed was necessary for every growing Christian. Understanding the propensity of self-centeredness (which leads to a lack of self-awareness), and the tenacious temptation to live isolated lives, Wesley instituted five levels of what he called "Christian conferencing." These were societies (similar to Sunday school classes designed for Christian education and instruction), class meetings (more on this later), bands (small groups), select societies (leadership development and mentoring), and penitent bands (recovery groups).

While all the levels of Christian conferencing were advantageous as a means of grace, Wesley came to believe that the class meeting was the heart of Christian community and vital to growing in Christlikeness. It became the "method" of the Methodist movement and, most maintain, was Wesley's greatest organizational contribution to the life of holiness. Its primary focus was not on Christian education, *per se*, but on behaviors, emphasizing the practical design and environment best suited for spiritual transformation. Bible studies and doctrinal teaching were important, but they were reserved for the societies. People were in class meetings to ask questions regarding the spiritual progress of each member. They were there to look each other in the eye and ask the question, "How goes it with your soul?" They were to hold each other accountable for growth in grace and offer whatever encouragement was needed to spur each other on toward holiness of heart and life.[41]

The most famous Protestant preacher in the eighteenth century was not John Wesley. That designation belonged to another Englishman, George Whitefield. An eloquent and dynamic preacher, Whitefield was universally considered the voice of Protestantism throughout the Western world and one of the prime movers of the Great Awakening in North America.[42] Wesley and Whitefield were close personal friends, and each admired the other's contribution to strengthen the church. But in the end, Wesley's work endured and not Whitefield's. Adam Clarke, a younger contemporary of Wesley, attributed the enduring fruit of the Wesleyan revival directly to the class meeting.

> From long experience, I know the propriety of Mr. Wesley's advice: "Establish class meetings wherever you preach and have attentive hearers; for, wherever we have preached without doing so, the word has been like seed by the wayside." It was by this means [of grace] we have been enabled to establish permanent and holy churches over the world. Mr. Wesley saw the necessity of this from the beginning. Mr. Whitefield . . . did not follow it. What was the consequence? The fruit of Mr. Whitefield's labor died with himself. Mr. Wesley's remains and multiplies.[43]

Whitefield himself, in response to a question about the impact of the Wesleyan revival, later reflected: "My brother Wesley acted wisely;

---

41. This section on the class meeting is adapted from my book on urban ministry. For greater detail on Christian conferencing and the impact of the class meeting on Methodism, see David A. Busic, *The City: Urban Churches in the Wesleyan-Holiness Tradition* (Kansas City, MO: The Foundry Publishing, 2020).

42. Harry S. Stout, *The Divine Dramatist: George Whitefield and the Rise of Modern Evangelicalism* (Grand Rapids: Eerdmans, 1991), xiii–xvi.

43. J. W. Etheridge, *The Life of the Rev. Adam Clarke* (New York: Carlton and Porter, 1859), 189.

the souls that were awakened under his ministry he joined in class [meetings], and thus preserved the fruits of his labor. This I neglected, and my people are a rope of sand."[44]

Discipleship can be personal, but it must not be private. Isolated Christians are in danger because insular faith produces weak and unfruitful disciples. Shared worship and Christian education are beneficial and necessary, yet without a shared life together of loving and intimate relationships, combined with the application of knowledge received, we will struggle to "work out our own salvation" (Phil. 2:12). The secret to healthy and happy growth in grace is in Wesley's repeated phrase "watching over one another in love."[45]

The Mercy of Self-Control

Learning to pray, fasting, Scripture reading, reflection, study, simplicity, solitude, submission, service, confession, worship, and relational accountability are all examples of the means of grace. These, and other spiritual disciplines like them, are part and parcel of sustaining grace.

You might say, "I don't have the aptitude for those things!" Join the club. The fact is that nobody has an aptitude for them at first. They are unglamorous and require hard work and ongoing practice. Do not forget, with the Spirit's help, our old nature is being transformed into a new one until what previously did not come naturally becomes second nature and "until Christ is formed in you" (Gal. 4:19). Perhaps that is why self-control is listed as the final characteristic of the fruit of the Spirit. Self-control is needed because the fruit is not automatic. The blossoms show the initial signs of potential,

---

44. Etheridge, *The Life of the Rev. Adam Clarke*, 189.
45. John Wesley, "The Nature, Design, and General Rules of the United Societies," *Works*, 9:69.

but apart from attuned concentration and deliberate attention, it is unlikely the fruit will mature.

Wright matter-of-factly makes the point that some fruit can be simulated: "All the varieties of fruit Paul mentions here are comparatively easy to counterfeit, especially in young, healthy, happy people—except self-control. If that isn't there, it's always worth asking whether the appearance of the other sorts of fruit is just that, an appearance, rather than a real sign of the Spirit's work."[46] No wonder, then, that self-control undergirds the resolute commitment to cultivating the life of holiness. "There are many parasites, many alien shrubs that will threaten to choke the fruit-bearing tree, many predators ready to nibble the roots or snatch the fruit before it ripens. There must be a conscious choice of mind, heart, and will to deal with all such enemies without mercy. . . . Just because you 'live in the Spirit,' that doesn't make following the Spirit's direction automatic. You have to choose to do it. And you can."[47]

Sustaining Grace: Spiritual and Practical

Sustaining grace is both spiritual and practical. It is spiritual in that it takes the Spirit. Just as physical fruit is the natural product of a living thing, so spiritual fruit is the product of the Holy Spirit. We cannot manufacture the deep work of God in us by the power of the Holy Spirit—it is that which comes from the outside and, as such, is utterly a gift. Yet it is also practical; quite simply, it takes practices. These practices take on the form of gardening so that what has begun in us will be "brought to completion" (Phil. 1:6) and "produce a harvest of righteousness" (v. 11). No farmer who plants corn on Monday expects to be eating corn on the cob the following Sunday. From seed to harvest requires cultivation and time. Water and sunlight are

---

46. Wright, *After You Believe*, 196.
47. Wright, *After You Believe*, 196–97.

necessary, fertilizer must be applied, and weeds must be tended to if we want to enjoy the benefits of fruition.

We are an instant-everything culture: instant coffee, microwave popcorn, and high-speed internet. People in coffee shops yell at their laptops if they take more than a few seconds to connect to Wi-Fi. The expectation of instant everything makes everyone impatient. Where does it come from? I maintain it is fueled by a more deeply rooted desire for instant gratification, which is not a modern phenomenon—it has been with the human race for a very long time. While there are many examples in Scripture of the deadly virus that is instant gratification, Esau—of birthright renown—is the most infamous. His sad reputation was settled after a long and unsuccessful day of hunting. When he returned to the home camp, he was famished. His cunning fraternal twin brother, Jacob, was preparing some red lentil stew over a fire. Esau demanded to eat. Ever calculating, Jacob negotiated a deal: "First sell me your birthright" (Gen. 25:31).

The birthright, or the right of the firstborn (also known as the law of primogeniture), was a common-law rule of inheritance that guaranteed financial privileges and family authority to the oldest male child—a prestigious and lucrative blessing. For Jacob to ask Esau to sell such a valuable possession for a bowl of soup was outrageous. Esau's response was equally outrageous: "I am about to die; of what use is a birthright to me?" (v. 32). He was willing to trade his most valued and treasured possession for a moment of instant gratification—quite literally, a bowl of red beans.

The irony cannot be ignored. What kind of impulsive person would trade something of infinite worth and inestimable value for a moment of instant gratification that will be over in a few moments? Yet our culture of instant gratification does it all the time: trades something of infinite worth and inestimable value for something they know is worth far less—something enduring for something short-lived. "I want what I want, and I want it now! I want my appetites to be met, even if it costs me everything." It is no wonder the writer to the Hebrews equates Esau's action with sinful immorality: "See to it that no one becomes like Esau, an immoral and godless person, who sold his birthright for a single meal. You know that later, when he wanted to inherit the blessing, he was rejected, for he found no chance to repent, even though he sought the blessing with tears" (Heb. 12:16–17). It is a tragic, hard-learned lesson that must not go unheeded. Discipline is required for the sanctified life, and one cannot short-circuit the process of discipleship.

Tiger Woods is acclaimed as one of history's greatest golfers. When I was a young man learning to golf, I tried to emulate his style. I wanted to hit monster drives like Tiger, strike my irons with pinpoint accuracy like Tiger, chip with a soft touch like Tiger, and putt with the confidence of Tiger (I even bought Nike golf hats to wear like Tiger). There was only one problem: Tiger practiced for hours every day, and had been since he was barely walking.[48] Even when he became the best golfer in the world, insiders tell us he still practiced harder than anyone else. I can say I want to play golf like Tiger Woods, but it means nothing unless my commitment to practice is commensurate with my desire. Instant gratification will not suffice. No matter how much I wish it could be different, my golf game is proportionate to my training commitment.

Sometimes people will say, "I want to be like Sister So-and-So. She seems so close to God. I see Jesus in her. She is a saint." It is not bad to see her as a good example of Christlikeness and seek to imitate her lifestyle, but what you may not know are the hours and hours she spends alone with the Lord in meditation and prayer—the decades she has spent on the spiritual practice range, being shaped

---

48. Woods appeared on *The Mike Douglas Show* to a nationally televised audience at the age of two.

into what you now see. She did not get to where she is by indulging in instant gratification. Spiritual practices have formed holy tempers in her that now look like virtue. She has gardened the fruit of the Spirit, and that is why love, joy, peace, patience, kindness, goodness, and self-control seem so obviously present.

Holiness is not a moment of time and *voila!*—virtue is acquired. No: it is what we are formed into. "Conversion is a gift and an achievement. It is the act of a moment and the work of a lifetime."[49] Patience for the long view is what is needed for the journey of grace. We must garden the fruit.

It feels only right to conclude a chapter on the enabling grace of God with a prayer for purity that has been prayed by the saints for more than a thousand years:

Almighty God, to you all hearts are open, all desires known, and from you no secrets are hid; cleanse the thoughts of our hearts by the inspiration of your Holy Spirit, that we may perfectly love you, and worthily magnify your holy Name; through Christ our Lord. Amen.[50]

---

49. Jones, *Conversion*, quoted in Foster and Smith, *Devotional Classics*, 281.
50. *The Book of Common Prayer* (Cambridge: Cambridge University Press, n.d.), 97–98.

6
SUFFICIENT GRACE

But he said to me, "My grace is sufficient for you,
for my power is made perfect in weakness."
—2 Corinthians 12:9, NIV

We started this book by saying that grace is personal, experienced, and known through the person and work of Jesus Christ, manifested in the presence of the Holy Spirit. As noted by Thomas Langford, grace is not known in the abstract as a principle, "but in God's actual self-giving in history."[1] In Jesus Christ and in the Spirit's presence, the renewal of human life is experienced through seeking, saving, sanctifying, and sustaining grace. This last biblical expression of grace is, for me, the most mysterious of all.

Have you ever wondered why those who appear to have an easy life can seem so distant from God, while those who are going through the deepest waters and dealing with the greatest personal struggles often sense the intimate nearness of God? At first glance, both observations appear counterintuitive. It stands to reason that those with

---

1. Thomas A. Langford, *Reflections on Grace* (Eugene, OR: Cascade Books, 2007), 107.

fewer problems would be happier and surrounded by greater peace than those enduring profound suffering, yet the opposite is often true. How do we explain such a paradox?

To pray, "Your will be done on earth as it is in heaven" is to confess that not everything that happens in the world is God's will. We do not attribute to God anything evil. Whenever we do, we impugn the character of God. The third commandment prohibits taking God's name in vain, which has less to do with cursing and more to do with misrepresenting God in the world. It is a serious thing to name anything that is evil as from God or to name anything that is from God as evil. Nevertheless, it should be mentioned that, even though not everything that happens is God's will, yet because our God is all-powerful and all-loving, God *has* a will in everything, especially as it relates to those God claims as his own and who abide in Christ.

Scripture reminds us that one of God's specialties is to redeem all things, even when evil is intended. Joseph said to his jealous brothers, "You intended to harm me, but God intended it for good to accomplish what is now being done, the saving of many lives" (Gen. 50:20). Again, Paul reminds us, "We know that in all things God works for the good of those who love him, who have been called according to his purpose" (Rom. 8:28). Joseph did not say God *caused* his brothers to sell him into Egyptian slavery; he said that God would not let their evil intentions have the last word. Paul did not say God causes bad things to happen to his people; rather, he said that God is faithful to work in everything, both good and bad, to take what appears to be only destructive and broken and make it healing and holy. These scriptures explain why those in Christ who face the greatest suffering are also the ones who experience the greatest peace. Something happens in the life of a fully consecrated disciple of Jesus who, along the journey of grace, goes through difficult circumstances and demanding situations. They experience God's sufficient grace in their weakness to sustain them and provide what is needed in their greatest struggles.

Strength Made Perfect in Weakness

The apostle Paul spoke about sufficient grace in the context of his second letter to the first-century church in Corinth. According to Paul, fourteen years before writing his letter to the Corinthians, he received a vision from God where he "was caught up to the third heaven" (2 Cor. 12:2). Most biblical scholars do not believe Paul was suggesting there are multiple levels of heaven but that he was describing a revelation beyond the ordinary human capacity to see and that he was able, by the inspiration of the Spirit, to perceive something beyond the physical realm. His point was to tell them, and us, that he had powerfully encountered the presence of God, had seen the risen Christ, and would never be the same—it had changed his life.[2]

Such a euphoric experience might cause one to be spiritually proud and boastful. Cognizant of the potential danger, and to keep from stumbling into unholy conceit, Paul adds that he was given a "thorn in the flesh" (v. 7). Neither the origin nor the specifics of the thorn are entirely clear. We do not know if the problem was physical, emotional, or relational.[3] What is clear is that it became such a heavy burden for Paul that he referred to it as "a messenger of Satan, to torment me" and remind him of his frailty (v. 7). He begged God to take it away, to remove his deficiency—and thus, it would seem, make him a stronger and better leader for the church. Before

---

2. Douglas Ward, "The 'Third Heaven,'" *The Voice: Biblical and Theological Resources for Growing Christians*, 2018, https://www.crivoice.org/thirdheaven.html. Many scholars maintain that the vision Paul describes in 2 Corinthians is a reference to his Damascus Road encounter with the risen Christ.

3. Some have speculated that Paul's thorn in the flesh was physical: a skin condition, acute vision problem, or epilepsy. Others have suggested the thorn was the memory of his past as a persecutor of the church and the relational difficulties that could ensue with the Jewish Christians.

we further explore the thorn, let us remember that Paul was a strong man. He was no spiritual weakling. In another place, Paul describes in detail his sufferings as an apostle:

> I've worked much harder, been jailed more often, beaten up more times than I can count, and at death's door time after time. I've been flogged five times with the Jews' thirty-nine lashes, beaten by Roman rods three times, pummeled with rocks once. I've been shipwrecked three times, and immersed in the open sea for a night and a day. In hard traveling year in and year out, I've had to ford rivers, fend off robbers, struggle with friends, struggle with foes. I've been at risk in the city, at risk in the country, endangered by desert sun and sea storm, and betrayed by those I thought were my brothers. I've known drudgery and hard labor, many a long and lonely night without sleep, many a missed meal, blasted by the cold, naked to the weather."

(2 Cor. 11:23–27, MSG)

Not to mention the ongoing pressure and anxiety of dealing with problematic churches and insufferable church members!

Read Paul's list of trials again. He endured all of that and undoubtedly more (snakebites come to mind). Are you convinced yet that Paul was neither a delicate flower nor a whiny complainer? This leads us to assume that whatever the thorn was, it was not an insignificant thing for Paul. No fewer than three times, Paul divulges, he appealed to God to take the thorn away (a biblical way of saying: "I just kept asking"). Paul is making us aware that he was in very deep water. He was carrying a burden that was crushing him, and he could feel himself stumbling under its weight. It was not a small thing in Paul's eyes, and he prayed for healing. The Lord answered his prayer but not in the way he expected. *No, Paul, you are going to keep the thorn, but know this:* "My grace is sufficient for you, for power is made perfect in weakness" (2 Cor. 12:9). *You are stronger in your weakest* moments when I am with you than you are in your strongest moments without me. *My strength is made perfect in your weakness.*

Carried in Divine Arms

Sufficient grace is the Lord's way of saying, *When you come to the end of your human strength, I will give you my supernatural strength. When your energy runs out, my energy will be made alive in you. When you cannot go any farther, I will pick you up and carry you. Rest in my arms for a while.*

There is a modern, well-known poetic parable called "Footprints in the Sand."

One night a man had a dream. He dreamed he was walking along the beach with the Lord. Across the sky flashed scenes from his life. For each scene he noticed two sets of footprints in the sand, one belonging to him and the other to the Lord.

When the last scene of his life flashed before him, he looked back at the footprints in the sand. He noticed that many times along the path of his life there was only one set of footprints. He also noticed that it happened at the very lowest and saddest times in his life.

This really bothered him, and he questioned the Lord about it. "Lord, you said that once I decided to follow you, you'd walk with me all the way. But I have noticed that during the most troublesome times in my life there is only one set of footprints. I don't understand why, when I needed you most, you would leave me."

The Lord replied, "My precious, precious child, I love you, and I would never leave you. During your times of trial and suffering, when you see only one set of footprints, it was then that I carried you."

If one could picture seeking grace in image form, it would look like a searching shepherd, a waiting father, an awakening kiss. If saving grace were an image, it would look like an embrace, an adoption, a reconciliation. If sufficient grace were an image, it would look like someone being carried in divine arms.

"Footprints in the Sand" is more than a parable—it is a real-life story I have heard over and over again. In my years as a pastor there were people in my congregations undergoing acute suffering and agonizing grief—some so severely I wondered how they had the strength to get out of bed in the morning; people so far at the end of their rope, to use Eugene Peterson's phrase, that "I could feel their desperation in my bones."

Then I would hear them say, "Pastor, I can't explain it. It doesn't make sense. I know I should be crushed by all of this, yet I feel"—and they would use these very words—"*as though I am being carried.* I am deeply saddened by this loss, this sickness, this death, this betrayal, and I should be falling apart, but there is a peace in my mind and a restfulness in my spirit that is unexplainable. The only way I can describe it is that it's like being graciously held up in everlasting arms." One set of footprints: sufficient grace.

If there is one thing I have discovered when it comes to suffering, it is that sufficient grace remains an intellectual reality until we need it most. One can know something in one's head and never know it in one's heart. To actually experience it, to be held up, to be carried, is beyond definition—it can only really be borne. Such is sufficient grace.

I was talking to a friend not long ago who said, "I don't know what I would do if I lost one of my kids. I wouldn't have the strength to go on."

I replied, "You are right. You don't have the strength right now because you haven't had to walk there. I hope you never have to, but if you ever did, there would be sufficient grace."

"Just Enough" Grace

Sufficient grace is whatever you need for today. It is a daily gift of "just enough." It is like manna in the wilderness. The people of God were on a journey through the desert. There was very little food, and, unless God provided, they were going to starve to death, so God gave them a gift. He rained down bread from heaven. Every morning when the people woke up it was on the ground outside their tents, baked fresh for that day. They did not strive for it, work for it, or pay for it. It was there as a gift from God's hand. All they had to do was collect and prepare it. The one stipulation was that they could not store it up. They could not stuff sweet pastries into a tin can and hoard them away for a rainy day. They could not hide manna under their mattresses just in case God did not come through the next day; if they tried, it would go bad. It would get wormy and fuzzy and turn into fish bait. They just had to believe that God would provide all that they needed today, and trust that God would do the same thing again tomorrow. His mercies are new every morning.

That is what sufficient grace is like. It cannot be stored up for tomorrow. It is sufficient for today. God gives us all we need today, and it is just right. Tomorrow will be just enough too. It is "whatever you need, I AM grace" that carries us when we cannot go any further. No wonder Paul confidently declared, "So, I will boast all the more gladly of my weaknesses, so that the power of Christ may dwell in me. Therefore I am content with weaknesses, insults, hardships, persecutions, and calamities for the sake of Christ; for whenever I am weak, then I am strong" (2 Cor. 12:9–10).

The Grace That Holds On

Some years ago, a pastor in Pennsylvania saw a man after church with a bulldog pin on his suit lapel. Not knowing that the man worked for a trucking company whose business logo was a bulldog, he naively asked, "What does that bulldog symbolize?"

With a twinkle in his eye, the man answered mischievously, "Well, Pastor, the bulldog symbolizes the tenacity with which I hold onto Jesus Christ."

The pastor replied, "It's a wonderful symbol—but bad theology."

Surprised, the man asked, "What do you mean?"

"It should never stand for the tenacity with which you hold onto Jesus Christ," observed the pastor. "It should stand for the tenacity with which Jesus Christ holds onto you."

Faith in difficult times is not a matter of how strong *we* are or how much faith *we* have. Faith in the darkest moments is really a matter of how strong God is. No matter what we encounter on the journey, God's grace is sufficient to hold us up, and his love is strong enough to pull us through it. Let us remember that the "no matter what" of life means that Jesus Christ is holding onto us with the tenacity of a bulldog and will never let us go.

A woman in a church I was pastoring suddenly became very ill. The doctors sent her through a gamut of tests to see what was wrong. They discovered she had a rare condition that caused her body to have severe allergic reactions to any food she ate. It became very serious, even life-threatening. During that time, her husband was deployed to Afghanistan to serve a tour of duty in the military. She was finally hospitalized and faced a medical test they expected would throw her into a violent allergic reaction that would cause her to temporarily stop breathing (similar to the anaphylactic shock that comes as a result of a peanut allergy). Nobody looks forward to such a violent reaction, especially when one knows it is coming. She told me, "Pastor, I was very scared, even to the point of panic. I was lying on the hospital bed, having a pity party about what I was about to endure, and wondering why all of this was happening to me. To top it all off, I was upset that my husband was thousands of miles away. I was afraid and felt very alone."

The time for the test came. She was terrified: "I now know what the term 'scared stiff' means. I literally couldn't move and I found that I could not even pray. I have never before not been able to pray. The only prayer I could muster was, 'God, please help me.'"

She turned to the nurse who was going to administer the test and asked, "Are you a Christian?"

"Yes, I am," answered the nurse.

"Would you pray for me?"

The nurse responded without hesitation, "Of course," and she proceeded to pray a simple prayer for comfort and healing.

My friend later told me, "As she was praying I had the most incredible peace come over me. It was almost as if God placed his hands on me and lifted me into his presence" (yes, she used that phrase). "I knew God was with me, and suddenly the fear was gone."

They administered the test, and to everyone's amazement, she did not have a violent reaction. "Pastor, I suddenly felt this wellspring of joy rising up in me. It was an exuberant joy. If I could have danced around the room, I would have!"

At that very moment, her nurse took off the radiation vest she'd been wearing, and there hanging around her neck was a large pendant cross.

Now with tears in her eyes from that vivid memory, my friend said to me, "That's when it dawned on me, God had been with me all the time—I just couldn't see him. I could not feel his presence, but he was there. He had been there all along. Though my husband was in Afghanistan, I was still the bride of Christ. Jesus was my husband at that moment, standing by my side, *carrying* me."

Along the journey of grace, God's sufficient grace holds onto us in a variety of ways, but one of the most important ways is through the body of Christ. It should not surprise us that, when we prayed for God to be revealed in our pain, it came in the form of a card or a phone call from a person in our church saying, "I love you. I am praying for you. The Lord is with you." We sometimes come into the fellowship of church carrying what seem to be unbearable burdens, and a brother or sister in Christ puts their arms around us and says, "You've been on my mind a lot as of late. I want you to know you are loved and prayed for." And, miracle of miracles, the incarnate presence of Jesus surrounds us, almost as if he were holding onto us in that moment with the tenacity of a bulldog, carrying us through the most challenging moments of our lives.

When one of my daughters was little, she was afraid of the dark. My wife and I would tuck her into bed and say, "Don't be afraid. Jesus is right here with you."

She would answer, "Okay, Mommy and Daddy. I won't be afraid."

But it was not long before we'd hear a knock on our bedroom door. "Mommy and Daddy, I know Jesus is with me, but I need someone who looks like you."

She was right. Sometimes we need someone who looks like us. That is what the body of Christ is—the Christian community is Jesus with skin on. Through the warm bodies of people, filled with his boundless compassion and enduring love, we are embraced and held up by God.

Endurance, Character, and Hope

Pain and suffering are things we usually want to avoid. It is not wrong to desire comfort and health. Yet we also know we can find joy, and even hope, in painful and distressing seasons because we know that Jesus's strength is made perfect in our weakness. In another letter to first-century Christians living in Rome, Paul said, "We also boast in our sufferings, knowing that suffering produces endurance, and endurance produces character, and character produces hope, and hope does not disappoint us, because God's love has been poured into our hearts through the Holy Spirit that has been given to us" (Romans 5:3–5). Once again, Paul is referencing virtue and character formation into the likeness of Christ.

First, suffering produces endurance. Problems, pressure, and trials are not random accidents of fate that have no bearing on our end goal (*telos*) of Christlikeness. In the original language of the New Testament, "endurance" is the word *hypomone* (hi-paw-muh-NAY), which means standing steadfast no matter what—standing firm even when the pressures of life come rushing in upon us. Difficulties produce endurance, and endurance is the quality that says, "I'm not going to quit, no matter what." It is similar to running a long distance. Your legs feel heavy, your lungs scream for air, your heart feels like it might explode out of your chest, and you badly want to quit. However, you know you have to keep running because, at the very moment when you want to quit, you are receiving the greatest fitness benefit. That is *hypomone*—endurance under pressure. We can rejoice in our problems and trials knowing that the pressures, and even sufferings, of life produce endurance and perseverance.

Second, endurance produces character. The Greek word *dokime* (doe-kee-MAY) originally referred to a metal that has been refined and had all the impurities removed. Problems and trials produce endurance, and endurance produces strength of character. At every level of society, character is desperately needed today. Richard John Neuhaus emphasizes the point: "That we are new beings in Christ is God's sheer gift; the construction of character is the actualization of that gift. It is a painstaking process of becoming who, in Christ, we already are. It requires respect for the everyday experiences, the quotidian [daily, ordinary] aspects, of the Christian's pilgrimage."[4] Neuhaus adamantly concludes: "Character implies the courage and grace to live the good life in a world where needs go largely unmet."[5] One does not receive strength of character by proxy. Prevailing through

---

4. Richard John Neuhaus, *Freedom for Ministry* (Grand Rapids: Eerdmans, 1979), 90.

5. Neuhaus, *Freedom for Ministry*, 88.

the tests of real-life situations produces endurance, and endurance, when made righteous, produces integrity and depth of character.

Third, character produces hope. Hope is the calm, certain belief that God is with us. Hope is the confident expectation that, no matter what the future holds, our journey-of-grace Companion holds the future. The central problem of our age is not too much stress but too little hope. Indeed, Thomas Langford states it well: "Hope does not defer to the future; hope reshapes the understanding of the past and determines life in the present. We live transformed in and by hope."[6]

An illustration may help clarify.[7] Imagine a room filled with high school seniors. You turn to the one on your left and ask, "How are you doing in your last year of high school?"

The student replies: "I am not doing very well. I failed several courses, and if I fail one more, I won't graduate. I'll have to repeat my senior year."

You ask again, "What do you see in your future?"

"Well, I'm *hoping* to graduate in May, and then I will try to get into a community college in the fall."

Then you turn to the student on your right and ask her the same question. "How are you doing in your senior year?"

"I'm doing pretty well," she says.

"Are you thinking of going to college?"

"Absolutely! I've already been accepted at Harvard. I'm still waiting to hear from Princeton, Stanford, and MIT, but I am *hopeful*."

"You must be a very good student. Would you mind telling me where you rank in your high school class?"

"Out of six hundred students, I am second in my class, with a 4.3 grade-point average."

---

6. Langford, *Reflections on Grace*, 107.
7. I heard this illustration in a sermon preached by Rev. Dr. Thomas Tewell in the 1990s called "The Tenacity of a Bulldog."

"Wow! That is impressive! Do you mind telling me how you did on your SAT?"

"I received a 780 in math and a 760 in language for a 1540 total." (800 is a perfect score in each category.)

"That's almost as well as I did on my SAT," you add wryly. "What do you see in your future?"

"Well, I hope to graduate in May and then go on to one of those universities to become a research scientist."

You think, *She **hopes** to graduate in May? This young woman has it made! It is not even a question.*

Do you see the difference? The first student was hoping beyond hope; the second student was hoping in certain confidence that it was going to happen. Hope such as this is not deferred to the future. It reshapes the understanding of the past and determines life in the present. We are transformed in and by hope like this. People sometimes say, "I *hope* God loves me. I *hope* God doesn't turn his back on me. I *hope* God doesn't abandon me when my back is up against the wall. I *hope* God will hold me up and strengthen me in my darkest hours." Christian hope is grounded in the past, present, and future love of the cross of Jesus Christ and the life-giving power of his resurrection. This hope does *not* disappoint us (Rom. 5:5). We are in the strong grip of God's sufficient grace. He holds onto us with the tenacity of a bulldog.

Into Your Hands, I Commit My Spirit

Not coincidentally, I wrote this chapter during the COVID-19 pandemic, a time of great uncertainty and profound suffering. Holy Saturday, the day before Easter, is intended as a time for quiet reflection on Jesus's death and remembering his time in the darkness of a tomb. One of the Lectionary texts for this day, Psalm 31, contained the words Jesus spoke from the cross before he died: "Father, into your hands I commit my spirit" (Luke 23:46). Jesus directly quoted Psalm 31:5, adding only the word *Abba* ("Father") to his prayer.

Of the many things to be learned from this prayer of Jesus, the one that stands out to me in the COVID-19 wilderness is that there is a vast difference between a life that is taken and a life that is given. Jesus made it clear in the Gospel of John: "No one takes my life from me, but I lay it down of my own accord" (10:18). He gives up his life freely and willingly. Jesus's death on the cross was not some tragic ending to a promising life or the disappointment of a failed mission. It was the divine design all along. The cross was God's cosmic plan to rescue us from the darkness and death grip of the principalities and powers. Thus, Jesus's sacrifice was not imposed on him—he willingly embraced it for us. He knew he was in God's hands, so he could say, "I lay down my life in order to take it up again" (10:17).

It should give us pause to ask, is our life being given or taken? There is a big difference between the two, mainly regarding the issue of trust. "Father, into your hands I commit my Spirit" means we trust that our life is being given for something bigger and more beautiful than we could ever accomplish apart from our heavenly Father. Jesus's praying that prayer at arguably the most difficult moment of his life tells us that he had already been praying this prayer for a long time—including the agonizing prayers he prayed in the garden of Gethsemane. "Into your hands" is a prayer of full surrender because, at its heart, it is a declaration that we are taking ourselves out of the hands of other people and circumstances—including our own plans and purposes—and willingly putting our lives into God's hands. In a powerful sense, it redefines and reimagines the experiences of our lives as either allowing things to happen to us or putting ourselves in the care of God to order our steps. One is to have something taken— the other is laying it down. It can be a loss or a surrender.

Jesus introduces us to the shocking power of sacrifice. He shows us that, by surrendering to God, we are able to turn something that *looks* for all the world like a loss into something that *is* for all the world a gain. When Frederick Buechner says, "To sacrifice something is to make it holy by giving it away for love," he means that even if someone is trying to pry it out of our hands, even when it feels like it is out of our control, we can still decide how we will let it go.[8] We can still open our hands at the last moment and give away what others thought was being taken from us and what circumstances seemed to be robbing from us. We can make it holy by doing it for love, by surrendering it to God.

In the surreal experience of the coronavirus pandemic, as days piled into weeks and weeks into months, it was easy to feel as if something was being taken from us. We felt scared, angry, uncertain, and way out of our comfort zones. We had a choice to make. We could play the victim and say, "Something was being taken from me," or we could surrender it to God and say, "Father, into your hands I commit my spirit. We surrender ourselves to your plans and purposes. Our lives are not our own. We lay them down because we belong to you, and we give them up for love so that you can make it holy." That takes some trust on our part, but the payoff is the absolute peace of knowing that our lives have glorified God, that our lives are not random accidents or failures of nerve but that our days are in his hands. Indeed, even in our suffering, we are held in his arms. Not even a global pandemic gets to dictate the purpose and meaning of our lives. No one takes our life—we lay it down. This is the reality of our hope.

---

8. Frederick Buechner, *Wishful Thinking: A Seeker's ABC* (New York: HarperOne, 1973), 101.

The Grace of Lament

Sufficient grace does not eliminate all our fear and doubt. There is no getting around it: even in hope there is room for questions. It is possible to have faith even when there are more questions than answers. It is possible to grieve and maintain hope at the same time. Not only is it possible—it is also biblical. We call it lament. Of the 150 psalms in the prayer book we call the Psalter, there are different varieties of psalms, including thanksgiving, royal, ascent, lament, and even imprecatory (prayers we pray when we are angry). The psalms offer us examples, as the inspired Word of God, of how to pray in any and every situation of life.

Psalms of thanksgiving (*hallel*—from where we get our word "hallelujah") are the prayers of praise we offer up when life is well ordered and God's presence feels especially near. Lament psalms, on the other hand, are the prayers we cry out to God in our pain, when life is hard and unsettled, with no end in sight. The two primary questions raised in lament are, "Why is this happening?" and "How long will this go on?" Not only does God allow these kinds of questions, but it is also interesting to note that 70 percent of the inventory of biblical psalms are pain prayers, not praise prayers—lament, not *hallel*. Jesus himself prayed a lament (Psalm 22) during his suffering on the cross.

The hallmark of lament is not doubt but deeply rooted confidence in the faithfulness of God. While lament can begin as a cry of desperation, its most important characteristic is profound trust in the nature, character, and power of God who is present in, participating in, and attentive to the darkness, weakness, and suffering of life. Lament is utter dependence on and total abandonment to a God who may seem distant but is never absent.

I have a friend who has been diagnosed with a rare form of cancer. Due to the uncommonness of the disease his doctors are trying various forms of therapy, many of which are experimental. Sadly, despite the best care and science available, cancer has continued to spread in his body. One day, after another bad report, his wife posted this testimony on Facebook: "While the medical treatment options are diminishing, the reality of God's presence is increasing." I do not know of a more beautiful expression of righteous lament and hope in the sufficient grace of God.

We are stronger in our weakest moments when the Lord is with us than our strongest moments without him. We have this assurance for the journey of grace: his strength is made perfect in our weakness. This is a hope that does not disappoint us. We will let Peter have the last word on sufficient grace: "And after you have suffered for a little while, the God of all grace, who has called you to his eternal glory in Christ, will himself restore, support, strengthen, and establish you" (1 Pet. 5:10).

AFTERWORD:
JESUS CHRIST IS LORD

*One life totally devoted to God is of more value
to Him than one hundred lives which have been
simply awakened by his Spirit.*
—Oswald Chambers

So much has changed in the last hundred years. Imagine being born in 1920, and being alive in the year 2020. In just a single century the cultural context in every region of the world has moved from industrial to information (Gutenberg to Google), from rural to urban, and from modern thinking to postmodern thinking. These are tectonic cultural shifts that remained unchanged in the previous five hundred years. What had been an environment of continuous change (that which is developed out of what has gone before and therefore can be expected, anticipated, and managed) for half a millennium quickly moved to a situation of rapid, discontinuous change that was disruptive and unanticipated.[1] We are in mostly uncharted waters.

---

1. Alan J. Roxburgh, *The Missional Leader: Equipping Your Church to Reach a Changing World* (San Francisco: Josey Bass, 2006), 7.

These foundation-shaking changes have generated new situations that challenge old presuppositions of how the world works. As a result, ecclesiology (the nature and structure of the church) and missiology (how the church engages the mission of God) by necessity have become highly adaptive without being compromised. In important respects, however, what remains constant in this time of rapid, discontinuous change is the eternal tenet that Jesus is the Way, the Truth, and the Life—or, in the words of the earliest Christian confession: "Jesus Christ is Lord."

Whom we deem "Lord" is a bedrock essential for the journey of grace. If we say, "[FILL IN THE BLANK] is 'lord'" (and it really doesn't matter whether it be another person, another thing, or oneself), it changes the entire narrative, including the ultimate goal and final outcome. But if we truly believe Jesus Christ *is* Lord, ordained to be so from everlasting to everlasting, there is only one rightful response: discipleship. Richard John Neuhaus reminds us that lordship is "not only an assertion of fact but a pledge of personal and communal allegiance."[2] Because Jesus Christ is Lord, we want to be like him. We want to do what Jesus did and live like he lived. That is the definition of Christian discipleship and is still the way Jesus gets into his church.

Dallas Willard makes the compelling argument that the New Testament is a collection of books *about* disciples, *by* disciples, and *for* disciples of Jesus Christ.[3] Thus, the goal of discipleship is not self-actualization ("I need to find my true self and what's best for me") or resignation to the forces of determinism ("I can't help it; that's just the way I am."). In fact, from the perspective of Christianity,

---

2. Neuhaus, *Freedom for Ministry*, 98.

3. Dallas Willard, *The Great Omission: Reclaiming Jesus's Essential Teachings on Discipleship* (New York: HarperCollins, 2006), 3. Willard reiterates that the word "disciple" occurs 269 times in the New Testament, while "Christian" is found 3 times and is introduced to refer precisely to disciples of Jesus in Antioch (see Acts 11:26).

being true to oneself is to be true to the self we are called by God the Father to be, remade in the likeness of his Son. Following Jesus and becoming like him is the unapologetic goal of the journey of grace. John the Gospel writer goes to great lengths to tell us that Jesus looks and acts like his Father: "Whoever has seen me has seen the Father" (14:9), and that Jesus is the Word made flesh and, having come from his Father, is full of grace and truth (1:14). Who Jesus is and what Jesus does are two sides of the same coin, a reality that raises important points for the nature of our discipleship.

Contrary to popular thinking, God is not a sentimental old man with a long, white beard who dismissively waves his hand and says, "It doesn't matter what they do; I just want the kids to enjoy themselves and have a good time." Neither is God the wrathful, harsh, angry Father who cannot wait for his children to mess up so he can vent his spleen and punish them. The first is grace without truth—soft indulgence without the fire of holiness, which leads to unaccountable permissiveness. The second is truth without grace—ruthless religiosity that leads to rigid legalism with little love. To be sure, it is not easy to maintain the balance between grace and truth, but they must be held in tension for the necessity and integrity of holy love.

Fundamentally, the fact that so many people in our churches are Christians in name but are not disciples of Jesus Christ who is Lord is the great problem of the church today. That consecrated discipleship (a life of learning how to live in the kingdom of God as Jesus did) has become optional except for the most radical among us is disastrous—not only because it perpetuates the idea that Jesus can be your Savior without being your Lord but, perhaps more importantly, because it assumes that grace is given to accept us as we are but has no bearing on what we become.

C. S. Lewis's observation that "the Christian does not think God will love us because we are good but that God will make us good because he loves us" is simply another way to say that God loves us as we are but loves us too much to leave us there. The love of God is holy love, so the kind of people we become matters to God. Holy love is full of grace and truth. Holy love dissipates cheap grace. Holy love becomes the condition and the means for discipleship. Holy love requires that we take up our cross and follow Jesus.

If taking up our cross seems like a difficult message for our time, consider the alternative: anemic and insipid existence lived for the self: religion without relationship. I have not been able to escape Dallas Willard's comments on the cost of "nondiscipleship" (his word):

> The cost of nondiscipleship is far greater . . . than the price paid to walk with Jesus. . . . Nondiscipleship costs abiding peace, a life penetrated throughout by love, faith that sees everything in light of God's overriding governance for good, hopefulness that stands firm in the most discouraging of circumstances, power to do what is right and withstand the forces of evil. In short, nondiscipleship costs you exactly that abundance of life Jesus said he came to bring (John 10:10). The cross-shaped yoke of Christ is after all an instrument of liberation and power to those who live in it with him and learn the meekness and lowliness of heart that brings rest to the soul.[4]

Discipleship is a journey of grace that begins and ends with Jesus, who is the Way, the Truth, and the Life. The goal of discipleship is to follow Jesus as we, by grace, become more and more like him. The journey is initiated and sustained by grace but is actualized as we freely cooperate with Jesus as Lord.

Christians are born; disciples are made. Christlikeness is our destiny; grace guides the journey.

---

4. Willard, *The Great Omission*, 8.